BRETTON WOODS:
THE FOUNDERS AND THE FUTURE

BRETTON WOODS:
THE FOUNDERS AND THE FUTURE

Edited by

Lawrence Goodman and Kurt Schuler

CENTER FOR FINANCIAL STABILITY

NEW YORK

Published 2019 by the Center for Financial Stability
1120 Avenue of the Americas, 4th floor, New York, NY 10036
http://www.centerforfinancialstability.org

Cover photograph by Britt Leckman
Cover design by Laneen Wells, Sublation Studio

ISBN 978-1-941801-07-9

Cataloging data will be available from the Library of Congress

Table of Contents

Introduction..1
Lawrence Goodman

1. Leadership and Strategic Vision at Bretton Woods..............3
Jacques de Larosière, Eric Helleiner, Eric Rauchway, Kurt Schuler, Spencer F. Eccles, Francisco Suárez, Yves-André Istel

2. Prospects for the World's Foreign Exchange System............10
Otmar Issing, John B. Taylor, Liu Mingkang, Charles Goodhart; Guillermo Ortiz, Peter Garber, Ronald McKinnon, Yu Yongding

3. Challenges for Advanced and Emerging Economies............20
Yves-André Istel, Adnan Akant, Takatoshi Ito, Richard Portes; Eduardo Aninat, Domingo Cavallo, Edward Offenbacher, Qiao Yide

4. The Future of Finance and Technology.........................26
Robin Lumsdaine, Sheila Bair, Charles Goodhart, Richard Sandor; Jack Malvey, Peter N. Johnson, Stephen Kealhofer, Dexter Senft

5. Crisis Management and Debt Restructuring.....................32
Robert Aliber, Paul Tucker, Nick Sargen, Lawrence Goodman; Robert Gray, Sean Hagan, Whitney Debevoise II, Richard Portes

6. The Future Role of the World Bank..............................38
Carole Brookins, Peter Woicke, Nancy Birdsall, Franco Passacantando

7. The Future Role of the IMF.....................................43
Randal K. Quarles, David DeRosa, Guillermo Ortiz, Siddarth Tiwari, Ted Truman, Tao Zhang; William Rhodes

8. Conclusion and Steps Forward...................................50
Randal K. Quarles, Ernesto Zedillo, Carole Brookins

List of Papers and Panels..57
Delegates..59

i

Acknowledgments

The Center for Financial Stability (CFS) thanks the Marriner S. Eccles Foundation, BNY Mellon, the Citrone Foundation, and the Y.A. Istel Foundation for their vision and support of the "Bretton Woods 2014: The Founders and the Future" conference.

We are grateful to the Bretton Woods Honorary and Steering Committee members, whose guidance and energy made our dive into the international monetary system a highly practical and deeply enriching experience. Members include Robert Z. Aliber, Eduardo Aninat(*), Bill Bradley(*), Carole Brookins(*), Jacques de Larosière, Barry Eichengreen, Charles Goodhart(*), Lawrence Goodman, Steve H. Hanke, Otmar Issing, Yves-André Istel, Takatoshi Ito, Henry Kaufman(*), Robin Lumsdaine, Jack Malvey, Guillermo Ortiz(*), Randal K. Quarles(*), William R. Rhodes, Richard L. Sandor(*), Kurt Schuler, John B. Taylor, and Yu Yongding.

Speakers and delegates liberally and often passionately contributed knowledge and perspective. We are grateful to them for their spirit. Their views are acknowledged throughout the monograph and they are listed at the end.

The CFS also thanks Marshall Wilen for his expert editorial advice and assistance.

(*) Current or former member of the CFS Advisory Board.

Introduction

Seventy-five years ago, 730 delegates from 44 countries got together in a resort hotel in Bretton Woods, New Hampshire, and accomplished something that had never been done before: They put into place an entirely new financial foundation for the world. These economic policymakers and thinkers envisioned a system that would foster growth, stability, and cooperation among nations. Their efforts to draw a roadmap for a secure, peaceful, and prosperous future in the midst of World War II remain memorable, and their achievement was evidenced by the growing prosperity and economic success experienced in the latter half of the 20th century.

Today, the global economy and financial system confront challenges of epic proportions. Central bank balance sheets are swollen to levels never seen before. Debt burdens are large and expanding rapidly. Many governments even earn revenue by borrowing, due to the prevalence of negative interest rates. Likewise, connections among nations are more tightly bound than ever before via financial markets, technology, and trade. It is no wonder that financial crises occur more frequently and with greater vengeance. In this environment, countries are increasingly guided by short-term interest. The system is frayed.

Institutions founded at the Bretton Woods Conference remain vital and at the heart of the global financial system. Yet, they are pressed by these challenges and are struggling to redefine themselves.

In 2014, some of the most prominent leaders from government, business, and academia gathered to commemorate the 70th anniversary of the Bretton Woods conference. "Bretton Woods: The Founders and the Future" was held at the same Mount Washington Resort, with the New Hampshire hotel exclusively available to the conference, as it was in 1944. The event, organized by the Center for Financial Stability (CFS), gathered the leaders in a working-group environment to better understand present challenges and offer solutions for the future.

The purpose of this monograph, which summarizes the 2014 conference, is to more broadly share seminal ideas and provide a springboard for offering practical strategies into the future.

After seventy-five years, issues remain. In fact, many have intensified and new ones have surfaced. The roots of the Bretton Woods agreements began more than twenty years before the agreements were reached in 1944, so we cannot expect today's challenges to be solved overnight.

Today, a new Bretton Woods may be impossible. Yet leaders would benefit from addressing hard questions that have been avoided for decades. Federal Reserve Vice Chairman and former CFS Advisory Board Member Randal K. Quarles closed the conference and perfectly captured the spirit of the group. The delegates were inspired, he told the assembly—inspired by the beautiful place, inspired by history, and inspired to go forward. But like the people in the Mount Washington ballroom over seven decades ago, today's delegates were mindful of the wise Greek proverb:

A society grows great when old people plant trees
whose shade they know they will never sit in.

Lawrence Goodman, President
Center for Financial Stability

Chapter 1

Leadership and Strategic Vision at Bretton Woods

Welcome

The Center for Financial Stability's 2014 conference at Bretton Woods began with an evocation of the 1944 conference and its results. **Jacques de Larosière,** who worked as a French financial official under the Bretton Woods system and later, as Managing Director of the International Monetary Fund from 1978 to 1987, dealt with post-Bretton Woods turbulence, sent remarks of welcome. He wrote:

> This [Bretton Woods] has been one of the rare moments in history where leaders got together to build a truly cooperative international order. This was the result of two essential factors:
> * A bold—but realistic—concept defined by the best economists of the time;
> * A visionary and comprehensive political leadership.
> The world prospered and economic growth expanded during the following 25 years. The Bretton Woods Agreement played a major role in these developments. But in the early 1970s, the Bretton Woods agreement collapsed, and we have witnessed, over the years, exchange rate volatility and misalignments, excessive debt, and capital flows that allowed the easy funding of persistent balance of payments disequilibria.
> Given the drawbacks of the present "anti-system," it is most appropriate to ponder and to work on what could be a new international monetary order.

Lawrence Goodman, president of the CFS, noted that "the deserved magic associated with Bretton Woods is about a shared long-term vision to avoid economic catastrophe and promote growth." Today, while the circumstances are not dire enough to forge a new Bretton Woods, "leaders would benefit from pulling a page from the 1944 playbook to think more strategically about the long term and the consequences of actions guided by short-term interest."

Recent Research on Bretton Woods 1944

Eric Helleiner, Eric Rauchway, and **Kurt Schuler** summarized recent historical research, including their own, in a short paper describing what new has been learned about Bretton Woods in recent years. They noted that the intellectual roots of the ideas that the conference crystallized went back much farther than is often appreciated. In 1913, John Maynard Keynes's first published book, *Indian Currency and Finance,* observed that in India, then a British colony, monetary officials maintained a stable but potentially adjustable exchange rate with the pound sterling by guaranteeing the sterling's convertibility into Indian rupees, but not the other way around, thus reducing their need for gold reserves. He argued that this practice was the future of monetary management. In 1919, at the Versailles peace conference, Keynes proposed a system of international lending for post-World War I reconstruction and development. This "grand scheme for the rehabilitation of Europe," as he called it, failed because the U.S. delegation declared that Congress would never back it. Keynes returned to idea of stable but adjustable exchange rates in his 1923 *Tract on Monetary Reform,* which criticized both deflation and inflation, but was harsher on deflation because of its typically more severe effects on employment. In his 1930 *Treatise on Money,* Keynes described the need for "management of the value of gold" by a "Supernational Bank" issuing an international currency in a system that would retain gold only as a "constitutional monarch"—keeping it for symbolic value but robbing it of actual authority. Thus, by the start of the Great Depression, Keynes had already proposed institutions that resembled the IMF and World Bank and had provided an intellectual underpinning for them. At Bretton Woods, he was the chairman of the "commission" (committee) on the World Bank.

In the United States, President Franklin Roosevelt and his administration adopted certain policies nationally that were forerunners of those agreed upon internationally at Bretton Woods. Roosevelt took the dollar off gold immediately upon taking office in March 1933 and secured the power to change the gold value of the dollar, within limits set by Congress. That power remained in effect until Congress approved the Bretton Woods agreements. Harry

Dexter White, who joined the U.S. Treasury Department in 1934, was involved with the U.S. coordination on exchange rate matters with Britain and France that began in 1936. He was also involved with U.S. government loans to Latin American countries in the late 1930s and with the abortive Inter-American Bank, which failed to secure approval from Congress. By December 1941, when he began drafting plans for what would become the IMF and World Bank, he had extensive relevant experience to draw upon. At Bretton Woods, White was chairman of the commission on the IMF.

At the Bretton Woods conference itself, an important finding of recent research was that what we would now call emerging markets had significant influence on the outcome. The United States was the leader, as the largest economy, and Britain was the No. 2 country at the conference because of its empire and Keynes's brainpower. Emerging market countries were, however, involved in drafting the IMF and World Bank agreements, and they persuaded the rich countries to make certain concessions to their views. They constituted a majority of the countries present, and in theory could have used the one-country, one-vote rule of the conference to pass provisions over the objections of the rich countries. In practice, the conference mostly used voting for final approval of understandings already reached by consensus. Working by consensus allowed the delegates to balance the realities that the United States, as the only large net creditor, would wield the greatest power at the IMF and World Bank, but that emerging markets could deny legitimacy to the institutions by refusing to join if they did not receive sufficient voice. The IMF and World Bank continue today to do much of their work by consensus.

Living Links to Bretton Woods 1944

The 2014 conference was fortunate to have in attendance several descendants of distinguished delegates to the 1944 conference, whose presence provided flesh and blood links from the past to the present.

Spencer F. Eccles, Chairman Emeritus of Wells Fargo Intermountain Banking Region in Salt Lake City, former CEO of First Security Corp. and a noted philanthropist, spoke about his uncle Marriner Eccles—who is often referred to as the father of the modern Federal Reserve. As chairman of the Federal Reserve System from

1934 to 1948, Eccles was the Federal Reserve's representative at the Bretton Woods Conference.

Marriner Eccles was the oldest child of Ellen Stoddard and David Eccles, a Scottish immigrant who became Utah's first millionaire. Marriner began working when he was only eight years old at his family's lumber company in a remote corner of Oregon. He ended his formal education after three years of high school and then served for two years as a Mormon missionary in Scotland. Soon after returning to the United States, his father suddenly died, leaving Marriner, then just 22 years old, in charge of the family's business interests as well as sharing responsibility with his mother for the upbringing of his eight younger siblings. As Spencer Eccles noted, "Marriner Eccles was an American original who brought to his participation at Bretton Woods a sense and a set of qualities—tenacity, plain-spokenness, chutzpah, and a willingness to lay aside pre-conceptions and follow ideas wherever they led—that our conference organizers hoped would help characterize our discussions here over the next couple of days.

"By 1928 he had expanded on his family's inherited share in his father's business interests, ultimately, acquiring 28 banks in Utah, Idaho, and Wyoming and with them as a nucleus, he formed First Security Corporation, the nation's first multi-state, actual operating bank holding company. Already his outside-the-box thinking and innovation was evident. Of course, just 18 months later, in October of 1929, the stock market crashed and the country fell into a deep depression. Marriner, with his young bank holding company and a number of other companies, was facing ruin and the loss of everything, everything his father had created and that he had built upon.

"Describing that crisis, Marriner said, and I quote, 'I awoke to find myself at the bottom of a pit without any known means of scaling its sheer sides.' He admitted that though he had been active in the world of finance and production for 17 years, he knew less than nothing about the overall economy. But again, he would not stand idly by and the wheels of his mind began turning. Going up against his very close older associates, whom he greatly respected, and who had assured him the terrible economic crisis was only temporary, and of course, going against the laissez-faire teachings of his father, he firmly decided that the depression wasn't just temporary, but long-lasting—critically long-lasting. He concluded that the only adequate source of strength that

6

could turn the economy upward was the federal government itself. And he called his theory 'compensatory fiscal and monetary policy'— that is, national deficits in depression, and surplus and debt repayment in boom times.

"Marriner proposed innovative new federal government deficit financing programs that later were to be coined part of the New Deal. So new were his ideas and his theory that many in the world of economics credit him with founding Keynes' theories before Keynes, whose general theory was not written until 1935 and which Marriner never read.

"But Marriner, was always driven by the facts even when the facts led to unexpected conclusions and he was not going to back down! As a result, this slight, middle-aged man from Utah, a Mormon, Republican banker, with no political experience but with solid commercial bank and business experience and with a plain speaking, get-things-done approach, attracted the attention of none other than President Franklin Roosevelt himself and his brain trust. The President made it clear he wanted Marriner to accept the chairmanship of the Federal Reserve. Obviously stunned, Marriner's answer was that at the bottom of the depression he could only leave his heavy banking responsibilities in Utah at this risky time and accept such an appointment if he could completely reorganize the Federal Reserve. He presented his plan, which was his outline of the Banking Act of 1935. No shortage of chutzpah here, eh? It must have been quite a thing in the White House office when that was presented to the President.

"But, ah, yes, let's not forget his homespun but ingenious method of addressing the so-called bank runs. Marriner's legendary creativity was routinely reprinted in textbooks for college students in courses on money and banking. Here's the crux of it, exactly as he managed it at First Security banks. On the first day of the bank run, he told the bank cashier and tellers, to carefully check each signature card, twice, and then, very slowly, pay off the deposits, with small bills. This continued throughout the first day and they announced that the bank would stay open as late as necessary. The next morning, they opened early and very quickly and efficiently paid off deposits with big bills, never letting a line form. And finally, be sure to bring in more currency from the Federal Reserve right through the bank lobby, in a flashy way, armored cars, police guards, assuring the depositors that there was plenty for everybody and much more where that came from. Of course, he didn't say that it wasn't the bank's money. And it worked. Not a single First Security Bank closed, and no depositor lost money, not a penny!

"So what does this mean for us here today? Well, today just as in Washington, D.C. of 1932 and Bretton Woods of 1944, we need people who are willing to set their preconceptions aside and follow the facts. We need people who are willing to think hard about the real world without the filters of theories they have grown comfortable with, whether those theories are from the left or from the right. and decide what the circumstances require.

"So who was Marriner Eccles? Well, I worked for him for over 25 years and I believe he was an example of the very best this country could ever produce. I hope this brief remembrance of one of the remarkable men who met here 70 years ago will help us all bring some of those same qualities to the questions of today—qualities we need now as never before."

Francisco Suárez Dávila is a former executive director of the IMF and at the time of the 2014 conference was Mexico's ambassador to Canada. He is the son of Eduardo Suárez, who was Mexico's minister of finance and the chairman at the 1944 conference of the commission that dealt with all matters other than the IMF and World Bank. For his father and for the Mexican delegation, explained Francisco Suárez, the main issue was the role that the Mexican delegation played, so that the World Bank should not only be concerned or primarily concerned with the reconstruction of Europe. Since the early meetings in Washington, the Mexican delegates fought for the inclusion of that goal. They had been frustrated earlier by their failure to create the Inter-American Bank, for which Mexico's central bank governor, Eduardo Villaseñor Angeles had presented a text as early as 1939, at a meeting of foreign ministers of the Americas. The agreement for the bank was signed in May 1940, but it didn't pass the U.S. Senate. However, Harry White was involved with it and drew some inspiration from it for his proposal of the World Bank. Francisco Suárez continued:

"In Commission II, chaired by Keynes, Mexico presented on the first day—as recorded in the memoirs of Suárez [and his fellow delegates] Cosío and Urquidi—a well-argued position that development should be included on equal footing with reconstruction.

Mexico argued in the commission's meetings of July 11 that 'in the very short run, reconstruction will be very urgent for the world as a whole, but in the long term, Mr. Chairman, before we are all dead, if I may say so [a clear reference to one of Keynes' texts], development must prevail.' Of course, history proved them right. The first loans were made to Denmark and France. After the Marshall Plan came into effect, development played the main role."

Francisco Suárez also addressed the current roles of the institutions founded at Bretton Woods. He said, "the World Bank has too much focus now on the poverty reduction role per se. Without a 'growth mindset,' it can easily become a type of Red Cross aid institution. The IMF can go back to being an adjustment police force....[T]he institutions require a major overhaul, not only plastic surgery."

For the remarks of **Yves-André Istel,** the son of André Istel of France, see chapter 3. Yves-André is an accomplished investment banker—serving as Senior Advisor and formerly Vice Chairman at Rothschild. Yves led the Bretton Woods group discussion and work on "Future Challenges for Advanced Economy Reserve Currencies." His brother Jacques-André Istel, a historian, Marine Corps veteran, and "the father of American skydiving," was also in attendance.

Chapter 2

Prospects for the World's Foreign Exchange System

Papers: Naughty or NICE?

Three papers and a panel discussed prospects for the world's foreign exchange systems.

Otmar Issing, former chief economist and member of the Executive Board of the European Central Bank from 1998 to 2006, and, more recently, head the German Federal Advisory Council on a New Financial Order, discussed "Future Prospects for the World's Foreign Exchange Rate System: Political Design vs. Evolution." He based his analysis on the "monetary trilemma."

In his words, "the monetary trilemma states that out of the three objectives—fixed exchange rate, capital mobility, and an independent monetary policy—only two of them are feasible at the same time. And with further increases in capital flows, a financial trilemma emerged, which I think is just paying tribute to the integration of capital markets. De facto, it is a dilemma because financial stability is the goal and financial integration and national financial policy are the elements which contribute to this goal or impede it. Financial integration can foster or endanger financial stability—depending, above all, on the soundness of domestic financial markets and institutions.

"Since the collapse of the Bretton Woods system in 1971/73, countries are free to choose their exchange rate system. They only have to notify the IMF of their decision. There are not even recommendations to be expected from the IMF, aside from special cases with programs. The choice is between many variants: We have the two corner solutions, [namely] hard pegs and free floating, and we have soft pegs, managed floats, and many variations of these different approaches."

Issing noted that free floating, while consistent with the trilemma, comes with the price of high potential volatility of exchange rates. In practice, the price may be too high for small economies, although they can reduce exchange rate volatility with capital controls, which are no longer taboo for policy makers, though they have dangers of their own. The currencies that are truly free floating are few: the US dollar, Japanese yen, pound sterling, Australian dollar, Canadian dollar, and euro. The euro is a special case, with one central bank for many sovereign states (18 in 2014, 19 in 2019).

Issing said, "European monetary union is an institutional arrangement which consists of member states which have transferred their sovereignty and monetary policy to the European Central Bank, a true European institution. And at the same time, member countries continue to be sovereign states in many respects. For this institutional arrangement, the no-bailout clause—which means that every country is responsible for its own policy mistakes and benefits—is an indispensable prerequisite. No country should be bailed-out by member states and the Union. However, this principle has been heavily violated time and again. The big question now arises whether the European monetary union will go back to the pure system of some sovereign states with their own currency or will evolve into a political union. [....]

"Political union for the time being will remain a vision, or whatever you would call it, for the more distant future. Almost no country in Europe is ready to give up its full sovereignty. I am afraid that we might enter into a mixture, that is to say a mess of fiscal union and European undemocratic decisions on fiscal policies, which will certainly not foster the way to political union. For some time to come, this will remain a very complex situation.

"There was a time when European integration and even monetary union was seen as an approach that might be a model to follow in other parts of the world. However, as long as Europe has not found a convincing, lasting response to the crisis, this has lost any appeal and acts rather as a discouraging example."

In the international monetary system, Issing expects the U.S. dollar to retain its dominant role because it combines deep, broad, and open financial markets with confidence in the future stability of the currency. Moreover, networks have developed around the dollar, and dislodging them would take time or a major shock. The IMF's Special Drawing Right and gold do not have these networks. The euro will continue to play an important role as an international currency. The position of the renmimbi will heavily depend on Chinese politics in the field of financial markets.

"So what will happen? I think a bipolar, tripolar, or even multipolar system might emerge, combined with the formation of currency zones around the leading currencies. For me, what is hard to predict is what the middle-sized countries and currencies will do in the future. Free floating?"

John B. Taylor, professor of economics at Stanford University and Under Secretary of the U.S. Treasury for International Affairs from 2001 to 2005, described a circumstance he called "NICE-Squared—Near an Internationally Cooperative Equilibrium." He observed,

"Soon after the end of the Bretton Woods system in the 1970s, monetary economists—myself included—started to use their brand-new Keynesian models with rational expectations and price rigidities to examine how monetary policy should be conducted in a world of flexible exchange rates. They found two surprising things.

"First, they found that simple steady-as-you-go, rule-like monetary policies would lead to a non-inflationary, consistently expansionary, or NICE outcome, to use the term coined by [former Bank of England governor] Mervyn King.

"Second, on the international side and even more surprising, they found that those same steady-as-you-go, rule-like monetary policies would also achieve most of the potential gains from international cooperation of monetary policy. And this would occur even if each central bank focused on its own country's economic performance. In other words, the international monetary system would be near an internationally cooperative equilibrium. One could say that the NICE system would help the world economy stay together during the NICE period. Let's just call it NICE-squared.

"What is even more surprising is that the actual outcome in the years that followed—the 1980s, 1990s, and until recently—seemed to bear out these NICE-squared predictions. As central banks moved toward more transparent, rules-based monetary policies—including through inflation-targeting—economic performance improved dramatically, especially compared with the 1970s. An important step was when the Fed began to announce its federal funds target.

"By choosing policies which worked well domestically, central banks contributed—in 'invisible hand'-like fashion—to better global economic conditions during this NICE-squared period. And toward the later part of this period, central banks in many emerging market countries began to move toward more rule-like policies. As they did so, they began contributing positively to overall global monetary stability."

In more recent years, international spillover effects have again become a major issue, particularly from U.S. monetary policy. Analyzing why, Taylor claimed that most obvious reason we are no longer in a NICE-squared world is that monetary policy deviated from rule-like policies. Taylor concluded,

"The implication is that we should try to go back to the steady-as-you-go, rule-like policies that worked in the NICE-squared period. An international understanding and agreement will help. Such an agreement could instruct the IMF or the BIS, or even ask private non-profit groups, to monitor the extent to which central bank policies are steady and rule-like.

"But will it be enough? I think so. The large destabilizing monetary-policy-induced capital flows motivated by search for yields would diminish. Fear of free-falling exchange rates would be calmed as reliable central bank actions come to be expected.

"A NICE-squared world would reappear. At least that is the hope and purpose of a conference like this."

Liu Mingkang, former deputy governor of the People's Bank of China from 2000 to 2002 and former chairman of the China Banking Regulatory Commission from 2003 to 2011, offered "A Few Thoughts on the Current International Monetary System." He remarked,

"Six years after the 2008 global financial crisis, the remaining financial market bubble that has not burst is likely the market for U.S. Treasury bonds and other G7 treasury bonds. What we are facing in the markets is an unstable equilibrium in the international monetary system with huge risks for the global economy. To these system weaknesses, we must do something quickly, even if they are still not very fundamental.

"In this case, what we must do is to make most of current opportunities.

1. National monetary policies should be better coordinated.
2. Information sharing and disclosure should be improved ...particularly through the IMF.
3. Capital movements should be carefully monitored and better managed...including through Tobin taxes in some cases.

4. Cooperation and coordination should be strengthened at all levels…through the IMF and the Financial Stability Board.
5. The role of a multi-currency system should be recognized in international trade and international payments. The dollar will not remain as dominant as it currently is, given the increasing importance of other countries in the world economy.

"In conclusion, in a risky and dynamic world, returning to the Bretton Woods System, or idly sticking to the current system, would be unwise. Higher-quality information, implementing standards and committing to sharing, better disclosure, fully fledged cooperation and coordination in deeds, and a refined financial governance system are the realistic solutions for all of us today.

"If we commit to working together now, through the strength of our combined efforts we may be able to create a more robust and flexible system that is capable of adapting to future changes. Conversely, the combined suspicions and panics of market actors may also result in amplified shocks and even greater challenges—an outcome that we must be ever vigilant for."

Charles Goodhart, a member of the Bank of England's Monetary Policy Committee from 1997 to 2000, asked the question, "The 1944 Keynes Plan: An Idea Whose Time Has Now Returned?" Comparing John Maynard Keynes's British plan for the post-World War II monetary system with Harry Dexter White's U.S. plan, Goodhart said,

"If you take the difference between the Keynes plan and the White plan, in my opinion, the difference was really fairly simple. The UK was a deficit country, and Keynes produced, I think, a quite outstandingly brilliant plan—I think the best plan that was ever produced along these lines—to try and make the adjustment process between deficit and surplus countries into a symmetric one, whereby the surplus countries had to adjust as much as the deficit countries did, under this system of bancor, an international clearing union approach.

"America, of course, was the biggest creditor country of all at that particular time and, therefore, Harry White was effectively determined that there were going to be no, or not any really very demanding, constraints on the surplus countries. So the IMF was born in a way that facilitated the adjustment of the deficit countries, and has never ever been really able to impose significant constraints on surplus countries, particularly large surplus countries. And to my mind, that has always been the great shortcoming of the IMF. All of the adjustment effectively is placed on deficit countries."

Goodhart noted that in the last few decades, some countries, including China, Germany, oil exporters, and until recently Japan, have had persistent current account surpluses, while others, notably the United States and United Kingdom, have had persistent deficits. He then speculated,

"In my view, all that is going to change, and change fairly dramatically, probably in the course of the next ten years, primarily because of demographic changes with an accompanying shift in the dependency ratio. It is quite likely that the current account surpluses of China and Germany and Japan will start shrinking really quite dramatically. It is also possible that if we can get on top of climate warming, that will involve, or it will have as an equivalent, a decline in hydrocarbon fuel prices. It could be that the world imbalances which we've grown to know, and not necessarily to love, over the last 20-30 years could be in the process of changing fairly sharply in the next ten years. And it may be that in about ten years' time, we won't actually know who are going to be the persistent credit account, surplus, or deficit countries.

"Now, if we were to be in a Rawlsian state of uncertainty about who is going to be in what position—so we don't actually know which countries are going to be running current account surpluses and which countries are going to be running current account deficits—and if the old order is changing, then we might be in a position all to agree, from a state of uncertainty, that it is actually desirable for those surplus countries to have to adjust as much as deficit countries are forced to adjust. It may be that there could be a window of opportunity, as the present structure of imbalances changes, for us to revisit the 1944 Bretton Woods arrangement and this time go for the British Keynesian approach."

Panel: International Monetary Prospects

Peter Garber, Ronald McKinnon, Yu Yongding, and Guillermo Ortiz (moderator) discussed "The International Monetary System: Alternative Perspectives and Prospects."

Guillermo Ortiz, former Mexican minister of finance and former governor of the Bank of Mexico, used his moderator's privilege to make two comments. The first was to define what is meant by the international monetary system. Following the IMF, Ortiz defined it as comprising exchange rates, payments for current transactions, international capital flows, and reserve accumulation. Clearly, in his view, the system, or "nonsystem," in place since the early 1970s, leaves something to be desired. It has suffered even more financial crises than the interwar system.

Ortiz's second comment was to note the Palais-Royal Initiative, a 2011 report by an international group of experts. Ortiz lamented that the group's proposals for international monetary reform could have been the basis for productive discussion by policymakers, but the euro area debt crisis entered a new phase shortly thereafter and dominated the attention of policymakers.

Peter Garber, global strategist at Deutsche Bank, discussed his work with Peter Dooley on the "revived Bretton Woods system," a concept they coined in a 2004 paper and had revisited in recent work. In an echo of the original Bretton Woods system, East Asian emerging markets, notably China, have de facto pegged their nominal exchange rates to the U.S. dollar, though individually and not under any multilateral agreement. They have promoted rapid export-oriented growth by keeping their real exchange rates undervalued, which has involved accumulating large dollar reserves through sterilized intervention and imposing capital controls. Eventually, though, they will need to liberalize their financial systems to move to the next phase of economic development, at which time floating rates would minimize disruptions.

In 2004, Garber and Dooley expected the revised Bretton Woods system to last ten or more years. Garber said that over the next several years, as the policies prescribed by the Chinese Communist Party's 2013 Third Plenum were implemented, the China phase of the revived Bretton Woods system would come to an end as China transitions to an open capital account and a flexible exchange rate. Other emerging market countries less developed than China, such as India, would keep the revived Bretton Woods system going beyond China's exit.

Garber termed China's large holdings of dollar reserves a kind of "hostage to Chinese good behavior" for foreign investment in China. Unlike a textbook developing country, China has been a large exporter of capital. The remarkably low real interest rates in advanced economies since 2000 would, Garber thought, continue until China liberalizes financially and floats its exchange rate, at which time its need for foreign reserves will diminish. Garber also warned that U.S. sanctions imposed on such major countries as Russia and Iran could move the international monetary system toward more closed arrangements like those of the 1930s, which would be undesirable.

Ronald McKinnon, professor of international economics at Stanford University (who died a month after the conference), stressed that despite many changes in outward appearance, "the world has been on a dollar standard since 1945." After World War II, the United States had the only smoothly functioning financial system and the dollar was the only major currency without exchange controls. Private exporters started invoicing their goods in dollars, and central banks held dollars to satisfy the demand of the private sector for foreign exchange.

McKinnon noted that U.S. policymakers have frequently complained about the large, persistent trade deficits that the United States has run. He maintained, in contrast to Peter Garber, that "it's the shortage of saving in the U.S. that caused the trade deficit, not the exchange rate."

On where to go from here, McKinnon advocated an agreement by the United States and China to stabilize the yuan-dollar rate. He would expect other Asian countries to peg to that rate without formal agreement as a way of stabilizing their own exchange rates. He was unsure whether the euro area would want to join, but would be happy if it did. The greatest benefit of widespread pegging, he thought, would be reduced flows of hot money resulting from expectations of nominal appreciation—another point on which he differed from Garber.

Yu Yongding, formerly a member of the Monetary Policy Committee of the People's Bank of China, discussed China's role in the international monetary system, and whether China's financial markets can become a source of global liquidity. He stated that China's growing weight in the world economy means that the renminbi will be able to play an important role, along with the U.S. dollar and the euro. He cautioned, however, that the internationalization of the renminbi "is a very long process. And I think the pace of internationalization may slow down in near future. So, if you want the RMB to come to rescue, it's possible, but not at this moment." China's financial reforms still have far to go. As an example, Yu cited the lack of a true benchmark interest rate comparable to the Federal Reserve's fed funds target rate. China has three benchmark rates, but none of them play a decisive role as a basis for the complex of interest rates. He also noted that without an open capital account, the renminbi will not become a truly international currency, though China has done more opening than people often realize. In his view, an open capital account also implies the need for a more flexible exchange rate.

Yu pointed out a kind of paradox, that "as a result of RMB internationalization, China's foreign exchange reserves increased, rather than decreased. In 2008, when RMB internationalization started, China's foreign exchange reserves were $2.4 trillion. Now it's more than $4 trillion," mostly in U.S. dollars.

Yu was pessimistic about the prospects for reforming the international monetary system in the short term. A global currency is politically dead for the time being. A multiple reserve system is possible, but as he had already explained, China was in fact reinforcing rather than supplanting the dollar. He did see some chance for the IMF's Special Drawing Right (SDR) to be used more widely, but in summary, "70 years after the Bretton Woods agreement, the situation has not changed very much" in terms of the dependence of the world financial system on the U.S. dollar, so the United States has a special responsibility to maintain a sound currency and sound financial system.

Guillermo Ortiz then invited **Ronald McKinnon** and Peter Garber to comment on the difference between their conceptual frameworks. McKinnon said, "The difference is, as I understand it, Peter thinks of undervaluation of currencies as generating a trade surplus with the periphery. And I think it was the fall of saving in the U.S. that generates the trade deficit. And that is endogenous because of the ease by which Americans can borrow in world markets; hence, personal saving is low. It has been disastrous for the fiscal stance of the [U.S.] federal government. The fact that savings deficiency shows up as a trade deficit has led to deindustrialization of the American economy. The creditors were big industrial countries back in the '80s, West Germany and Japan, but now China and a group of quite highly industrialized Asian countries are the creditors. Americans must do something to get their saving rate up strongly, and it'd be helpful if China moved more toward consumption-based economy to keep the balance here."

18

Yu Yongding remarked that he disagreed that deliberate undervaluation of the renminbi was a wise policy, because it was by definition a misallocation of resources.

Peter Garber said that it is hard to tell whether capital inflows to the United States are "pulled" by low U.S. saving or "pushed" by emerging markets desiring to save in dollars. Very low long-term real interest rates in the world are a clue that "push" factors are dominant. Garber also said he did not think a world system of pegged exchange rates would be viable in the absence of renewed capital controls.

In response to questions from the audience, **Yu Yongding** elaborated a bit on how use of the SDR might be promoted. **Peter Garber** and **Yu** said they did not expect the World Trade Organization to have any important role in the debate over the international monetary system, and Yu said that China should let the internationalization of the renminbi emerge from the markets rather than push it hard as a matter of policy.

Chapter 3

Challenges for Advanced and Emerging Economies

Panel: Future Challenges for Advanced Economy Reserve Currencies

Yves-André Istel, senior advisor and former vice chairman of Rothschild, Inc., moderated a panel with Adnan Akant, Takatoshi Ito, and Richard Portes. Istel set the stage by enumerating the characteristics that major reserve currencies have historically had. Two—sufficient quantity and efficient capital markets—are anodyne, but Istel also noted that the major reserve currencies over the last several centuries have been currencies of leading military powers. He questioned whether the euro can ever rival the dollar as long as multiple sovereign credits fragment its market. A multipolar international monetary system might come into being, but only over a long period.

Adnan Akant, head of foreign exchange at Fischer Francis Trees and Watts, spoke from his experience as a trader and a manager of reserves for central banks. The key weaknesses he saw in the current international monetary system were the inadequate supply of safe assets for the demand and the lack of an adjustment mechanism for global imbalances other than financial crisis.

Reviewing the prospects of the major currencies, he saw no good alternative to the U.S. dollar in the near to medium term. The negative real interest rates of the dollar and the large trade and federal government budget deficits of the United States are weaknesses, but its demographics and growth prospects are favorable for an advanced economy. In addition, it will remain the major military power. The euro area has strong fundamentals in many areas but its lack of growth is a big weak point. As its members move toward greater integration, the euro might provide a model for how to achieve a global currency. Akant thought that the Japanese yen would shrink in importance because Japan has very high government debt. The Special Drawing Right (SDR) is not the currency of any one country, and it is unlikely to replace national currencies. That leaves the Chinese yuan, but for reasons discussed by Yu Yongding in the previous panel, Akant did not expect the yuan to displace the dollar soon. Finally, he noted that in the market, "we do see central banks moving away from the dollar and adding carry trades and also moving towards sovereign wealth funds because that is one way of solving the Triffin [safe asset] dilemma." (See below for more discussion of it.)

Takatoshi Ito, former member of the Economic and Fiscal Council of the Japanese Ministry of Finance, noted that no Japanese delegation was present at Bretton Woods in 1944 because "we were on the other side of the fence. So I apologize." To help think about the prospects for currencies moving up to reserve currency status, like the U.S. dollar, euro, pound sterling, and Japanese yen, he asked why the yen had remained a secondary reserve currency and had not become a regional reserve currency in East Asia in the 1980s and 1990s, when Japan's economic influence in the region was at its postwar height. He attributed it to the Japanese government's lack of interest in pushing to internationalize the yen or to establish regional monetary institutions in Asia that would not be as subject to U.S. influence as the IMF. Also, Japanese companies that expanded abroad learned how to work in multiple currencies.

China, in contrast, is making a much stronger push to internationalize the renminbi. China's growing economic influence means that, looking ahead over the next 70 years, Ito expected it will become a major reserve currency. The yen, he thought, would not be absorbed into a renminbi bloc, and would have a similar relation as the pound sterling has to the euro. His biggest concern for the future is whether China will remain within the institutions and arrangements that originated at Bretton Woods, or would instead try to challenge them and create a parallel system.

Richard Portes, professor of economics at London Business School, spoke about the "Triffin dilemma" and its relevance to the present. Robert Triffin, a Belgian-American economist, claimed in testimony to the U.S. Congress in 1959 and in a book in 1960 that increasing demand for dollar assets would strain the ability of the United States to supply sufficient dollar assets while maintaining the dollar's peg to gold. Either the United States would fail to provide sufficient dollars and a deflationary global liquidity shortage would ensue, or the increasing accumulation of dollar holdings abroad would undermine confidence in the dollar.

In Portes's view, though, "the dollar problem of the 1960s was not founded on the Triffin dilemma; it was the result of the U.S. inability to convince dollar holders that the U.S. would maintain a stable value of the dollar with appropriate monetary and fiscal policies....I would argue that the Bretton Woods exchange rate mechanism broke down mainly because of the expansion of capital flows, rather than loss of confidence in the dollar."

Portes thought that even if one believes that something like the Triffin dilemma is happening today in the form of a shortage of safe assets, the system will adjust. "The supply will go up and the demand for them long term will go down. There will be a multipolar reserve system, not because of the Triffin dilemma and the shortage of safe assets, but because official reserve holders want to diversify their portfolios." Countries with large official reserves will invest some of the reserves in sovereign wealth funds, which can trade off higher risk for higher return. And emerging markets will develop their domestic financial markets and have less need for foreign intermediation.

Panel: Emerging Markets: New Reserve Currencies and Spillovers from Advanced Economies

Eduardo Aninat, former deputy managing director of the IMF, moderated a panel with Domingo Cavallo, Edward Offenbacher, and Qiao Yide. Aninat suggested an analogy between currencies and languages as networks, and noted the complexities that can arise from making abrupt sudden changes to exchange rate systems.

Qiao Yide, Vice Chairman of the Shanghai Development Research Foundation, asked, "What is the purpose of the international monetary system?" He proposed that "it is to provide global liquidity in accordance of the needs of global economic growth." There is a global liquidity imbalance due to more and more financing occurring across borders, but liquidity provision remains national. Moreover, emerging markets obtained a growing share of the world economy, now comprising more than half of world GDP, but liquidity provision remains concentrated in the advanced economies, particularly in the United States.

Qiao then discussed some means of reducing global liquidity imbalances. He noted that private institutions have played an increasing role by offering greater cross-border financing. He remarked on the way that central bank swap lines provided liquidity during the global financial crisis. Regional financial arrangements, such as the Chiang Mai Initiative in Asia, are another way of providing liquidity. Finally, a move away from the U.S. dollar as the dominant global currency would also reduce liquidity imbalances by providing more channels for liquidity.

Domingo Cavallo, former Argentine minister of the economy, observed that "the main advantage of getting the status of reserve currencies is the fact that then the country can issue all its debt in local currency. That is why more and more countries will continue to try to make their currencies eligible for reserves, or at least to get this property. By the way, the reason why I agree, also, that the Chinese will not be moving urgently towards making the renminbi a convertible currency and a reserve currency is because as a creditor country, a net creditor country, they do not get significant advantages. On the contrary, if moving towards convertible and reserve currency causes the renminbi to appreciate a lot, that could even create sort of deflation in their tradable sectors and create insolvency in the Chinese banks."

Recalling John Taylor's presentation (Chapter 2), Cavallo claimed that at least since 2004, the monetary policies of the advanced economies had not been NICE, particularly for emerging markets. "Emerging markets have a double curse. Their currencies are not trustworthy enough to be reserve currencies, and they suffer from spillover effects from the domestic policies of the advance countries." Consequently, they have a more limited menu of options than advanced economies for using domestic policies to fix imported problems.

Financial crises and sovereign debt crises are the consequences of excessive indebtedness in one or more sectors. Advanced economies can issue domestic-currency debt to bail out debtors. This strategy, however, can create inflationary problems immediately in emerging markets and eventually in the advanced economies. A better way, Cavallo thought, was debt restructuring.

Emerging markets live under the shadow of advanced economies' currencies, but in Cavallo's view, where foreign currency is widely used domestically, the best course "is to accept the competition of foreign currency and manage monetary policy in order to increase the trust in their local currencies." Forced conversion of foreign currency into

23

local currency does not solve underlying policy problems, as Argentina found out in 2002. Some emerging markets may wish to go to nondiscretionary monetary policies and establish currency boards or dollarize.

As for steps to improve the international monetary system, Cavallo proposed improved bank resolution in advanced and emerging economies alike; a sovereign debt restructuring mechanism such as Anne Krueger proposed in 2001 when she was first deputy managing director of the IMF, or at least improved collective action clauses in new bond issues; and an increased role for the IMF as a lender of last resort. Cavallo also approved of Ronald McKinnon's suggestion of a stable dollar-yuan exchange rate as a basis for convergence by other countries.

Edward Offenbacher, a member of the management board of the Bank of Israel, discussed the difficulty of assessing interest rate fundamentals to determine whether low real interest rates are the consequence of being in the NICE world John Taylor described, or whether they result from policy-induced distortions ("currency wars").

Offenbacher reminded the audience of Taylor's BIS working paper of December 2013, in which Taylor spoke about two periods prior to the 2018 global financial crisis when the outcomes were quite positive. There was asset cooperation between countries, with each country following Taylor-type flexible inflation targeting. Through asset cooperation, Offenbacher noted, countries had achieved a "sort of Nash equilibrium in the macroeconomic outcomes of the world economy." Then the global financial crisis hit, leading to unusually low central bank policy rates. This "ultra-easy monetary policy" among advanced economies, Offenbacher pointed out, was generally followed by similar policies in the Successful Emerging Market Economies (SEMEs). Taylor presented two alternative explanations for the lower interest rates: Either lower interest rates are driven by currency wars— in which countries found themselves in a monetary version of the Prisoner's Dilemma. If everyone would be less expansionary, everybody would better off. But an individual country that is less expansionary than others will get hurt a lot more. So, countries began to violate the near-international cooperation equilibrium by engaging in currency wars. On the other hand, perhaps the driving force is fundamentals, meaning the natural rate of interest is falling.

Which explanation is the key driver of monetary policy? Offenbacher proposed that because it is extremely difficult to get agreement among decision makers as to what the fundamentals are, there is a strong bias towards the currency war story among policy decision-makers.

Offenbacher used Israel as a typical case in point to explain the difficulties of low world interest rates for its monetary policymaking. Israel should be among the world's best candidates for a fundamentals-based story, yet Israel is heavily influenced by the currency war story. The Bank of Israel's policy rate at the time of the conference was 25 basis points, the lowest in history, even though strong fundamentals such as healthy growth, a current account surplus, the discovery of large natural gas deposits, strong increases in house prices, and inflation greater than the advanced country average suggest that the rate should be higher. Offenbacher concluded that "the key takeaway from my ideas here is that the macroeconomic policy advisors need to figure out how to do a much better job of explaining the fundamental stories to the policy decision makers. If interest rates are too low relative to [fundamentals] for too long, global financial stability may well be at stake."

In the question period, **Ted Truman,** a former Federal Reserve official, commented that "the Federal Reserve, too, lives within a much more integrated globalized world than it used to be and, therefore, it has no choice but to take account of that."

George Hoguet, an emerging markets portfolio manager at State Street Global Advisors, asked **Domingo Cavallo** why some countries are more heavily de facto dollarized than others and hence more subject to buffeting from changes in U.S. monetary policy. Cavallo replied that "the countries that are highly dollarized have not chosen to be highly dollarized, but their history, particularly of hyperinflation or a monetary regime's collapse…created an ad hoc dollarization. Once you have an ad hoc dollarization, the only way to stabilize the economy is to allow people to continue using the dollar as an alternative to the domestic, currently. If you just prohibit the use of the foreign currency, and you force the people to use the local currency, what you will create are black markets and then nobody will trust in your currency." He cited Peru as a country where competition with the dollar has promoted good monetary policy and confidence in the local currency, which had been lost during a hyperinflation.

Chapter 4

The Future of Finance and Technology

Panel: The Future of Finance and Financial Institutions

Robin Lumsdaine, senior fellow at the Center for Financial Stability and professor of international finance at American University, moderated a panel consisting of Sheila Bair, Charles Goodhart, and Richard Sandor (who was unable to attend, but sent comments for Lumsdaine to read).

Sheila Bair, former chair of the Federal Deposit Insurance Corporation, discussed how she thought the evolving regulatory framework was affecting the financial services industry and markets now and how it would in the future. She expressed her disappointment with the focus of policy in the United States during the global financial crisis. In her view, the bailouts focused too much on banks and not enough on overleveraged homeowners, who dramatically cut their consumption to keep paying their home loans, creating problems for industries dependent on domestic consumer demand.

She wanted a financial system that was simpler, smaller, less interconnected, less leveraged, more consumer-focused—one that would not need to be bailed out. She saw some progress in the form of tougher capital rules, many of which have not yet gone into effect, however. She also remarked, "the rules themselves are making the industry more complex, not less. And I also think we're starting to segue into an environment where the biggest banks will continue their market dominance as the smaller banks struggle with the regulatory costs, which are disproportionate for them because of their smaller financial resources."

She added, "I think the regulators have lost confidence in market discipline. I think that is the problem. They are trying to substitute for the lack of market discipline with a very, very highly prescriptive rule and supervisory process. And, again, I think this is destined to failure. In my view, the best kinds of regulations are the ones that reinforce market discipline." Her fear was of "highly prescriptive rules and [a] very intensive supervisory process, and, again, bailouts being entrenched as a paradigm in place of the forward-looking paradigm of restored market discipline and a ban on bailouts." She wanted a system that can take prudent risks but would have plenty of capital to cover losses when risks go bad.

Charles Goodhart, a former member of the Bank of England's Monetary Policy Committee, focused on two topics: housing finance and the use of cash.

Mortgage finance by banks involves a maturity mismatch: Borrowers want to borrow for long periods and lenders want to be able to draw down their bank deposits on demand. Although he favored increasing banks' equity ratios, he noted that European regulators made a big error in raising the ratios without giving thought to where the equity would come from. Many banks responded by reducing their mortgage loans and other credits (the denominator in the equity ratio) rather than by increasing their equity (the numerator).

Moreover, Goodhart said, "Each national government has turned to its own domicile of national banks, and said, 'Although we want you to de-lever in order to increase your equity ratios, we don't want you to cut back in lending into your own country.' The result has been an absolutely dramatic decline in cross-border lending. And the decline in cross-border lending has led to the fragmentation and balkanization of the European financial system, and to a degree, of the world financial system."

American regulators have made a different kind of error, failing to reform the housing finance commensurately with reforms of banking finance. Goodhart suggested Danish-style "covered bonds" or "shared equity mortgages," where the lender gets some of the appreciation potential in return for a lower down payment, as possible ways of reducing the maturity mismatch.

Turning to the use of cash (notes and coins), he remarked, "We haven't had any significant technological change for several centuries. Indeed, with coins, apart from the fact that the edge of coins began to be milled around two centuries ago, the technology actually goes back millennia." He stressed that cash is a magnet for crime, and that it facilitates illegal activity. Purely electronic payment, however, has the disadvantage of lacking anonymity. His suggestion was for a pseudonymous electronic money, such as has been proposed by David Birch in the book *Identity is the New Currency*. Under Birch's system, the veil of anonymity would only be breached if the authorities could convince a judge to do so.

Goodhart also noted both the possibility of paying a positive rate of interest on government-issued electronic money as a way of encouraging people to switch out of cash, and the possibility of a negative rate of interest to escape from the zero lower bound on interest rates when it threatens to cause or extend recessions.

Richard Sandor, CEO of American Financial Exchange (AFX), had two remarks he wished to pass along. One was to ask whether a new Bretton Woods must look to the East. The other was to note "legislation inflation." The bill that established the Federal Reserve was 25 pages long. The bill that established the Commodities Futures Trading Commission was 148 pages long. In contrast, Dodd-Frank was 2000 pages long, more than the Old Testament, the New Testament, and the Koran together.

In the question period, **Stanley Black,** professor of economics at the University of North Carolina, asked **Sheila Bair** to comment on the balance between regulation and lawsuits as a means of ensuring bank soundness. Bair responded that "a robust enforcement process is really key to ensuring accountability in a changing behavior. I guess on that, I would not give a very high score to our efforts in the U.S."

Eric Stein from Eaton Vance asked **Sheila Bair** how policymakers convince markets that they will not continue with bailouts. Bair said that for money market mutual funds, floating the net asset value rather than pegging it at $1 per share would make it plain that they are mutual funds, not banks. Regarding banks, Bair wanted to see better "living will" planning and issuance of contingent convertible debt. **Charles Goodhart** demurred, saying that such measures might well just shift losses around the financial system without ultimately changing it.

Panel: Technology and the Future of the International Financial System

Jack Malvey, chief global market strategist at BNY Mellon, moderated a panel with Peter N. Johnson, Stephen Kealhofer, and Dexter Senft. Malvey noted the effect of technological changes on finance by asking, "What do you think has had a bigger impact in the financial system, Microsoft or the financial system framework?"

Developments in artificial intelligence have the potential for huge further changes in the not-too-distant future.

Peter N. Johnson, vice president of enterprise application and information services at MetLife, had two key points. The first was, "You ain't seen nothin' yet" when it comes to data analysis. "The second half of the story around big data…is the passive data that you generate or the machine-generated data as the world becomes instrumented. This is the data that's thrown off by your cell phone as you're walking around. This is the data that's thrown off by your automobile as you travel"—in other words, data generated passively, rather than actively such as when conducting an online search. Looking forward 70 years, the world will be highly "instrumented" (a wide range of devices will be linked to immense data analysis capacity), with an emphasis on instant decision making and transactions.

Johnson's second point was, "Just because you hire a smart team of data scientists doesn't mean you're going to get a great business result." In making use of big data, creative business thinking is more important than the technical engineering and mathematical skills involved. "The data can answer the questions. The data can help generalize from the past and help predict the future, but it's the creative business leadership that has to frame the questions."

Dexter Senft, co-head of electronic markets at Morgan Stanley, observed that equity markets were virtually all electronic; futures markets are nearly so; and electronic trading was coming into foreign exchange, fixed income securities, and mortgages. However, "the very biggest tickets and the majority of the volume are still done by human beings. Why is that? Well, that's because the machines aren't very good at anticipating how markets will react to large-size transactions. If a transaction is big enough to move the market, then you want the kind of intelligence that only an experienced human trader can give."

Transparency and liquidity are often inversely correlated. "Transparency is fantastic for the liquidity of small transactions" because machines thrive on predictability, but "it can be quite harmful to the liquidity of large transactions because the person who needs to step in and provide the capital to get that large transaction done is usually not very keen on having the whole world know that he just did it. The whole world will now be competing with him to transact the hedge that he's about to execute because he did that trade."

Government policy with respect to electronic markets needs to recognize that tradeoff.

Stephen Kealhofer, managing principal of DCI, an investment management firm, talked about how technology affects what firms like his do. He listed four desiderata in financial markets: accurate prices, allocative efficiency, low costs, and wide access. Generally, going from institutionally intermediated exchange to market-intermediated exchange moves markets closer to the desiderata.

Stock index futures and trading in credit-default swap (CDS) indexes, which require less capital than holding the underlying assets, have boosted market liquidity of the underlying assets. During the Great Recession, Kealhofer explained, "bond trading was very difficult. You could get it done but it was hard. Most of the big dealers withdrew. Most of the people trading bonds were relying basically on brokerage. The regional brokers came to the fore in that period of time. But what traded continuously and quite well throughout the entire crisis was the single-name CDS. And the reason was you didn't have this gigantic capital requirement behind it."

Kealhofer's final point was that "innovation in credit is really driving the average credit quality down. So, the stress on intermediation in credit increases if you're actually doing financial innovation right. If you're getting more people into the market, you're creating more access. It's increasing the amount of credit risk in the system. Is that good or bad? In my view it's good but you need to have a good intermediation process for it." Markets such as the credit-default swap market enable the kind of credit intermediation that is necessary in such a system.

In the question period, **Jack Malvey** asked **Peter Johnson** how quantum computing changes things. Johnson replied that quantum computing, while important, will not be as important as the development of networks. He expected Metcalf's Law, which says that the value of a network grows as the square of the number of participants in it, to be more significant than Moore's Law, which posits that the number of transistors on an integrated circuit doubles about every two years.

Jack Malvey asked **Dexter Senft** how computerized trading changes employment for traders. Senft replied that over the previous 20 years, total employment on the trading side remained just about unchanged but the nature of the jobs changed, involving greater skill or working more with machines to make machines smarter at what they do. **Malvey** also asked **Senft** whether electronic trading will help liquidity provision in credit markets. Senft said, "The way I would have you think about it is that electronic trading is a highway for assets to get from one place to another. The balance sheet is the parking lot where bonds spend the night on their travels....But the highways themselves will not be enough, so we're going to need to get more balance sheet from someplace."

Jack Malvey asked **Stephen Kealhofer** whether in the future, portfolio management will be conducted mainly by artificial intelligence. Kealhofter answered yes, citing the ability of machines to find patterns and exploit anomalies much faster than humans.

Charles Kimball of the Korea Center for International Finance asked "what the flash crash of the future might look like." **Dexter Senft** said, "I think what you will have when the whole ecosystem reaches the right degree of sophistication is that the accidents will create small craters, not large ones," but that vulnerability to hacking, rather than innocent errors, would be a risk.

Stanley Black, professor of economics at the University of North Carolina, asked whether big data offers a solution to a reduction of U.S. federal government collection of certain economic data. **Dexter Senft** pointed out that government-collected data tend to be lagging and backward-looking, and that big data offers the promise of much more detailed, real-time data.

Kurt Schuler, senior fellow in financial history at the Center for Financial Stability, asked about the implications of bitcoin and other crypto-currencies. **Dexter Senft** answered that he was "very, very bullish" on Bitcoin with an upper-case B, the blockchain technology and protocol, but not so bullish on bitcoin with a lower-case B, the cryptocurrency.

Chapter 5
Crisis Management and Debt Restructuring

Panel: How to Better Anticipate and Manage Future Crises

Lawrence Goodman, president of the Center for Financial Stability, moderated a panel with Robert Aliber, Nick Sargen, and Paul Tucker. Goodman asked the panelists to consider what went wrong during the global financial crisis and what recommendations they had.

Robert Aliber, the coauthor, with the late Charles Kindleberger, of the renowned *Manias, Panics, and Crashes: A History of Financial Crises,* made four points. The first was that banking crises have certain regularities. Those of the last 30 years were all preceded by capital inflows, leading to rising security prices and, if the exchange rate floated, an appreciating exchange rate. Some borrowers were using new loans to pay off interest on old loans. Lenders realized what was happening and ceased new loans, and some borrowers then defaulted.

Aliber's second point was that Lehman Brothers was a victim of the end of the credit cycle. "The source of the problem," he said, "is essentially that there is too much credit and the private lenders are simply just the channels of the distribution of credit. We have these crises always at the end of periods of very, very rapid credit growth when the supply of credit is very cheap."

His third point was that, regrettably, his former colleagues at the University of Chicago, Milton Friedman and Harry Johnson, "got it very wrong" when they imagined in the 1950s and 1960s how a system of widespread floating exchange rates would behave. "The international financial system is dysfunctional, and we need to somehow change the institutional arrangements."

Finally, regulation is costly and it has not prevented serious crises. He challenged the regulators in the room to answer the question, "Why has the last 200 years of regulation been so ineffective in preventing the crisis of 2008? Let's find out the answer to that question before we adopt more regulations. Thank you very much."

Paul Tucker, former deputy governor of the Bank of England, argued that the crisis of 2008-09 was so bad because "the major financial institutions and banks generally had almost no tangible common equity capital." The international minimum equity requirement for tangible common equity at the time of the crisis was below 1 percent of risk-weighted assets. If the average risk weight was about 50 percent, it meant that the implicit leverage limit was above 200 to 1, so not much had to go wrong for collapse to ensue. The pre-crisis Basel regime was misleading (and deeply flawed) because "capital" could include hybrid securities that could not absorb losses in a going concern. The crisis was so severe "because the world woke up to the fact that banks had precious little tangible common equity." Policymakers have not increased tangible equity requirements to the double-digit levels suggested by some economists because "they didn't know what the consequences would be on credit supply. Which is where Bob [Aliber] ended."

Nick Sargen, chief economist of Fort Washington Investment, summarized the financial crisis as "the intersection of three events": a housing bubble and excess credit leading to mispriced credit risk, which Sargen perceived at the time, and the vulnerability of the largest financial institutions, which he did not. The financial institutions that went bankrupt or required assistance held a high percentage of toxic assets, bad asset/liability mismatches, and high leverage.

There were warning signals in August 2007, when central banks injected liquidity to respond to the problems of structure investment vehicles (SIVs); in March 2008, when Bear Stearns failed; and subsequently, when there was discussion about what would be the next notable financial institution to fail.

The 2008-09 crisis was not the first near-death event for the financial system. The Third World debt crisis of the 1980s threatened to capsize some banks. They had the advantage of not having to mark their securities to market. Banks and policymakers had time to reflect and act. What happens when securitized finance speeds up events, though? Policymakers have to make instantaneous decisions. The developers of securitized finance did not envision that it would be used to securitize low-quality mortgages. "Basically, instead of the system dispersing risk and having diversification, the system spread risk, and that's why I think that securitization contributed...to the severity of the crisis."

In the question period, **Lawrence Goodman** asked, based on the assessments the panelists had made of what went wrong, what to do to better manage and help prevent crises. **Paul Tucker** asserted that post-crisis reforms to financial regulation had gone pretty well, but "a static rules-based system will not work because a fact of life is that regulatory arbitrage is endemic and finance is a shape shifter." Hence, the problem of shadow banking. Rather, "we need a world of constrained discretion just as we have in monetary policy." (Tucker has since written a book on this subject, *Unelected Power: The Quest for Legitimacy in Central Banking and the Regulatory State.*) He also argued that efforts to reform the international monetary system faced the insuperable difficulty that surplus countries, especially when powerful, never agree to bear their share of adjustment, whereas deficit countries have no choice. Even if surplus countries did agree, they might well later renege. Tucker also said that the IMF needs to make analysis of mismatches and other vulnerabilities in national balance sheets, encompassing the private and public sectors, central to what it does.

Robert Aliber stressed the connection between large capital inflows and banking crises that have followed. The economy must adjust to absorb these real resources. Changes resulting from these inflows "are much sharper under floating exchange rates because there is a feedback effect, an accelerator, [from] the money inflows into rates of return. We see this in the very sharp, much sharper, changes in the ratios of current account balances to GDPs when currencies are floating than when they're pegged....The impacts of cross-border investment flows on household wealth and consumption spending are much sharper than the impacts of changes in monetary policy."

Nick Sargen disagreed in part with Aliber's view of capital flows as pushed rather than pulled into countries. He said, "there are periods in which the primary driver of international capital flows is changes in monetary policies," which create interest rate differentials that investors respond to. Policymakers need to understand what the effects of their policies may be on the flows. Sargen also said, "I would say that today, in making investment decisions, the most important part is risk assessment rather than investment opportunity."

The audience then asked questions or made comments in a single round, to which the panelists responded in a single round. **Roger Farmer,** professor of economics at the University of California, Los Angeles, suggested that huge swings in ratios such as price to earnings "are signals that the markets are not allocating capital in the way that our theories tell us that they should. Developing mechanisms that go much beyond simply thinking about capital ratios and potentially to trying to stabilize those ratios, are things that I'd like to put out there as a radical suggestion for the way that we move policy forward." **Madelyn Antoncic,** vice president and treasurer of the World Bank, remarked that financial regulation should be based on what firms do rather than whether they are incorporated as banks, insurance companies, etc. She also expressed skepticism about the value of "living wills" for financial institutions. **Yves-André Istel,** senior advisor and former vice chairman of Rothschild, Inc., observed that, in part because capital movements are not as large proportionally, Americans policymakers resist principles-based regulation such as Paul Tucker advocated, favoring rules-based regulation instead. **Joel Motley** of Public Capital Advisors asked whether a situation such as the 2008 U.S. debate about whether to buy toxic assets from banks or inject new capital into them was too complex for predetermined rules, lending support to Paul Tucker's preference for principles-based regulation.

Robert Aliber remarked about the crisis that "one of the lessons is that we know too little about the relationships between liquidity- and solvency-type issues. Essentially what happened [is] liquidity dried up and firms that on Monday were thought to be solvent, on Tuesday were underwater." Second, "the further down the road of regulation we go, the greater the incentives we will develop for an unregulated sector," which, if significant enough, gets bailed out.

Paul Tucker responded to Joel Motley by saying that if you know which assets are toxic, buying them is not a completely crazy policy; but if you don't, it is crazy. A capital injection absorbs losses wherever they come from, and benefits from leverage. On living wills, he stressed that he does not think their American version, which is about using regular bankruptcy proceedings for large financial institutions, can work. The version he has in mind, which is a short statement of how an institution can be handled if it comes under the resolution powers of regulators, is feasible, not least because it makes cross-border cooperation easier as everyone knows in advance whom they will be cooperating with. Finally, he said, "In order to sustain the same desired degree of resilience, what we need from our legislators and from society is for them to tell us what degree of resilience against systemic stress they want."

Nick Sargen remarked, "The big question for me is, show me when regulators have ever been countercyclical as opposed to being pro cyclical. I think it's just the inherent behavioral issue."

Panel: The Future of Sovereign Debt Restructuring

Robert Gray, chairman of Debt Finance and Advisory at HSBC Bank, led a panel comprising Sean Hagan, Whitney Debevoise II, and Richard Portes. Gray observed that after several years out of the limelight, sovereign debt restricting was back in it because of problems in Argentina and especially Greece. He asked the panel to consider whether sovereign debt restructurings have been timely enough; how restructuring should happen, including the use of aggregated voting by creditor; and what role the IMF should play.

Sean Hagan, general counsel and director of the Legal Department at the IMF at the time, offered his views, speaking in a purely personal capacity. He viewed sovereign debt restructuring as having two big issues: "When should you restructure? And secondly, having decided to go ahead and do it, how do you proceed?" Most governments only come to the IMF after they have lost access to the market. "So, the key issue for the Fund at that point when they've lost market access is, are we going to provide financing to support a program that enables them to service their obligations, or is our program going to be contingent upon some form of debt restructuring." Since 2001, the IMF's position has been that unless repayment of the debt seems highly sustainable, "when in doubt, there's going to have to be a restructuring."

Now that holdings of sovereign debt are no longer concentrated in a small number of banks but dispersed among many investors, coordinating collective action is harder. Moreover, courts in recent years have strengthened the position of holdout creditors by partly rolling back sovereign immunity. Creditors no longer need to find assets to attach; they only need to find a stream of payments and enjoin the sovereign from paying them.

Whitney Debevoise II, senior partner at Arnold & Porter Kaye Scholer LLP and former U.S. executive director at the World Bank, spoke in a purely personal capacity. He said, "I think of sovereign debt restructuring as a three-legged stool, the three legs being the degree of economic adjustment by the country that has the problem, the possibility of official sector financing....And then the possibility of debt restructuring by various creditors....The real question is how do we create incentives for the relevant factors involved with each one of these three legs of the stool."

Direct negotiation with private creditors of an economic adjustment program does not work well; the IMF's role as a third party is valuable here. To fulfill that role best, the IMF needs seniority as a creditor, de facto if not de jure. In debt restructuring, "the essential question here is how do we find the market clearing price?" Collective action clauses make it easier to find such a price for sovereign bonds. Debevoise noted, though, that, "I also see creeping back into sovereign finance more syndicated lending, more project financing, other types of claims" that do not have such clauses. "So, at the end of the day, we may have aggregated one class of creditors, and that will be useful, but we may not have solved the entire problem. So that's something for people to work on going forward."

Richard Portes, professor of economics at the London Business School, observed that his research with Barry Eichengreen on sovereign defaults in the interwar period found that internal rates of return on loans that defaulted averaged 2 percent, even after taking the defaults into account. Other researchers studying other kinds of credit to sovereigns and other periods have found similar results. So, despite problems, sovereign lending does not turn out too poorly.

Portes then discussed the euro area in particular. Several countries have high levels of debt that will remain high if growth remains sluggish. "Part of the stagnation and threat of deflation is due to inadequate monetary and fiscal stimulus in my view, but I think part of it is also due to the debt overhang. Those who are familiar with the Latin American debt crisis will recall the 'lost decade,' which didn't yield to a resumption of growth until the Brady plan finally cut the debt to manageable levels. High debt is a tax on investment and growth." In place of the existing policy of "extend and pretend" on debt, Portes favored a policy of debt reduction by capitalizing the seigniorage receipts of highly indebted euro area countries.

In the question period, **Gary Kleiman** of Kleiman International observed that "external corporate activity is now dwarfing traditional sovereign borrowing. Much of that is quasi sovereign. We saw it in the Dubai case [Dubai World, 2009] that there aren't really any good workout mechanisms in that regard."

Chapter 6
The Future Role of the World Bank

Carole Brookins, former U.S. executive director at the World Bank, moderated a panel with Peter Woicke, Nancy Birdsall, and Franco Passacantando. She began with a brief review of the organization and evolution of the World Bank. The World Bank Group today comprises the bank itself (International Bank for Reconstruction and Development, IBRD) plus four newer entities: the International Finance Corporation (IFC); the Multilateral Investment Guarantee Agency (MIGA); the International Development Association (IDA); and the International Centre for Settlement of Investment Disputes (ICSID). They reflect "the institution's shifting priorities and the decisions made over the years by the bank's leadership and the member countries....The menu gets longer every year, with new priorities. So over these years we've known the reconstruction bank, the infrastructure bank, the structural adjustment bank, the knowledge bank, and now President [Jim Yong] Kim says the Bank is the solutions bank." The World Bank Group is now involved in an enormous range of issues, from its original focus on project lending to the business investment climate, rural development and sustainable agriculture, women's roles in societies, debt forgiveness, education, healthcare, sanctions on minerals and mining and "global public goods"—advising countries on trade negotiations and now the big issue of climate change and the environment.

Peter Woicke, former managing director and executive vice president of the International Finance Corporation, noted that during his years there (1999-2005), he was surprised by the skeptical attitude of World Bank Group toward private sector development and to the reluctance of its employees to rock the boat, for instance by speaking up to contradict their managers. He thought that the attitude towards private sector development had changed since he left, but according to his sources, the reluctance of employees to rock the boat has not.

"When the Bank focused on things, I think successes were very visible," Woicke said, citing Asia, especially South Korea, after the regional financial crisis of 1997-98; the Balkan crisis; and privatization in Eastern Europe. With regard to the World Bank's efforts to disseminate knowledge, Woicke cited the Annual Development

Report; the Doing Business Report; and the guidelines the Bank has developed with regard to various investment, social, and environmental issues. He added that, however, some aspects of capacity building were still lacking and offered examples.

Nancy Birdsall, founding president of the Center for Global Development and a former manager at the World Bank, offered three wishes for the World Bank. The first was to return to the growth-oriented spirit of its founders and avoid turning the Bank into a poverty reduction agency, which is not its strength; in this, she agreed with the criticism Francisco Suárez Davila made in his speech. The founders of the World Bank and IMF had a few brilliant ideas. One was that the Bank could be "a global credit cooperative," able to borrow at lower interest rates than most of its members and to pass the savings along. Another was weighted voting by members, which helped the IMF and World Bank reflect the realities of power in the world economy and make them more effective than a one-country, one-vote scheme would have. Another brilliant idea, which, however, has not been put into practice, was that the World Bank could provide countercyclical finance.

Birdsall's second wish was for the World Bank to play a greater role in providing and coordinating global public goods. After 70 years, the Bank is still focused on loans and guarantees: "They're all country-focused." To move the Bank towards a more global role, a president of the World Bank or a major shareholder (probably the United States or China) would need to say that the Bank needs a new mandate from its members and the money to support it.

Her third wish was for the United States to support the World Bank better. The United States was a "benign bully, and I emphasize benign, in creating a liberal international order until maybe ten years ago." But it has since been neglectful, as seen in particular by the small proportional increase in the World Bank's recent capital increase compared to those of the regional development banks, even "after the global financial crisis woke up everybody to the logic that these banks could use effectively somewhat more resources." The United States should move "away from a benign bully, dad role, [and] a little bit more to consensus building again, and let the Chinese in [to greater influence], as many people have said." Finally, Birdsall criticized mandates on U.S. action at the World Bank imposed by the U.S. Congress at the behest of nongovernmental organizations, which are well intentioned but can constrain the future of the developing countries.

Franco Passacantando, formerly an executive director of the World Bank and a manager at the Banca d'Italia, noted that at the time of the Bretton Woods conference, private markets in international capital were almost nonexistent and the world was much poorer. Now that private capital markets are robust and poverty has been greatly reduced, is the World Bank still needed? He answered that it was, partly to deal with failed states or other countries in great difficulty, but more importantly, to contribute to policies that foster growth by helping borrowing countries develop policies that place project lending by the Bank in the most effective context. He also remarked that the nature of poverty is changing: There are fewer countries where almost everyone is poor; poverty in the future will be located in middle-income countries.

Carole Brookins asked the panelists two major questions: Has the World Bank been successful as builder of capacity in local institutions—if not, what does it need to do? The other question was how to transfer knowledge from one place to another to allow scalability.

Peter Woicke said, "I think the World Bank Group has failed in providing the governance because basically shareholders love projects. They don't like long-term investments," such as building healthcare systems. China, however, was a significant exception: "China has taken advantage, and I mean this in a positive sense, of the World Bank as very few other countries have." **Nancy Birdsall** maintained that governance is "not something you can beat on or build up....Now, sometimes you get a great political leader who really steps up, but for the most part it's not something you can do from outside." She suggested outcomes-based aid as a way of working around governance problems to some extent.

In response to a question by **Carole Brookins** on the World Bank's internal governance, **Franco Passacantando** offered a European counterpart to one of Nancy Birdsall's wishes, wishing that Europe could reduce its representation on the executive board from seven directors to two, one for the euro area countries and one for the rest. **Peter Woicke** wanted an executive board that acted more like a corporate board of directors, not resident in Washington and not deeply involved in internal governance, but rather holding managers to what they have promised to deliver.

In questions from the audience, **Daniel Runde,** former director of the Office of Global Development Alliances at the U.S. Agency for International Development, asked how to divide labor between the World Bank and the regional development banks; what role the IFC should play in the future; and to what extent the World Bank should focus on failed or post-conflict states. **Franco Passacantando** replied that no clear rule about division of labor is possible, but that coordination could be improved. **Peter Woicke** said that that IFC is bringing in the private sector, not crowding it out. **Nancy Birdsall** said that in post-conflict and failed states, "the World Bank has a role there, absolutely. Indeed, its comparative advantage is to work in those countries, because it looks at all sectors and reforms."

Bob Aliber claimed that the "World Bank is essentially a monopoly. How should I know whether it deserves additional resources, whether it uses resources wisely?" Where is the cost-benefit analysis? **Madelyn Antoncic,** vice president and treasurer of the World Bank, asked how to make appropriate changes, particularly to overcome risk aversion by World Bank employees. **Mahesh Kotecha,** president of Structured Credit International Corporation, pushing back on Peter Woicke's comment, asked why the World Bank couldn't collaborate more systematically with regional development banks and the private sector.

Peter Woicke, responding to Aliber, said the World Bank did not need more resources; it needed to reallocate them to the most effective channels. "I think the IFC should use the profits they're making today to fund venture capital in poor countries for entrepreneurs. The money is there but it's been transferred into IDA. The IFC is making money on the back of the private sector, giving to IDA, and that IDA money disappears in corrupt governments." **Nancy Birdsall** and **Franco Passacantando** noted that the World Bank is not a monopoly; similar financing is available from the regional development banks. Birdsall agreed with Woicke that the IDA should shrink and the Bank's "hard lending window" should grow.

To an audience question about corruption in projects, **Peter Woicke** suggested that a way around it would be for the World Bank to be able to lend directly to local governments or even nongovernmental organizations. **Nancy Birdsall** asked, "What does 'zero tolerance' for corruption—what message does it send to staff? Be careful. Avoid risk. Don't do any projects that might later generate noise about corruption. Don't do anything where you're not covered."

Carole Brookins asked the panelists to state one or two priorities the World Bank should focus on between now, 70 years after Bretton Woods, and 70 years from now that would contribute to raising living standards and growth in developing/emerging countries?

Franco Passacantando suggested leveraging the large amounts of private sector and official funds looking for investment outlets. **Nancy Birdsall** proposed to return to the spirit of the founders of the IMF and World Bank by broadening governance, allowing China, Brazil, and other emerging markets more influence, so that there is more of a sense that the institutions are not just run by the advanced economies. **Peter Woicke** reiterated his remark that the executive directors should act more like the board of a firm, giving the staff more freedom in return for holding managers more accountable for results.

Chapter 7
The Future Role of the IMF

Panel: The Future Role of the IMF

Randal K. Quarles, former undersecretary for domestic finance of the U.S. Treasury Department and former U.S. executive director at the IMF, moderated a panel with David DeRosa, Siddharth Tiwari, Edwin (Ted) Truman, and Tao Zhang. Quarles noted that the IMF, though it no longer supervises the Bretton Woods system of pegged exchange rates, has not reinvented itself as often as the World Bank. He also noted some of its possible missions: crisis manager, global liquidity manager, upholder of macroeconomic policy standards, exchange rate adviser, early warner of vulnerabilities, think tank.

David DeRosa, president of DeRosa Research and Trading, said of the IMF, "I think that basically its *raison d'être* ended in 1971 or '73, depending on whether you date it from closing the gold window or for the wholesale abandonment of the Bretton Woods exchange rate regime, and I think that since then, it's tried its best to come up with very important things to do. One thing it did do is it created quite a pool of talent."

Guillermo Ortiz, former Mexican minister of finance and former governor of the Bank of Mexico, saw at least two useful roles for the IMF. As a crisis manager "during the Latin American crisis of the '80s, the Fund actually was instrumental in preserving, I would say, the health of the banking system worldwide, obviously at the cost of Latin America....And then during the emerging market crisis of the '90s starting with the Mexican crisis, [it] played a very useful role." (Ortiz was appointed minister of finance shortly after the crisis began.) Another useful role for the IMF is as the center for global financial cooperation. Ortiz thought that the G20 should be merged with the IMF's International Monetary and Financial Committee to make the combined body effective and powerful. He also suggested that member countries give the IMF a remit concerning the global capital account, to get the IMF more involved in issues of global liquidity, and that the remit extend both to capital exporters and capital importers.

He recommended that the United States support an increase of IMF quotas.

Ted Truman, senior fellow at the Peterson Institute for International Economics and a former official of the Federal Reserve Board of Governors and the U.S. Treasury Department, said, "the overarching objective of the Fund has been its international monetary cooperation role, and that role has evolved over time." When problems have arisen, such as high oil prices in the 1970s, Third World debt in the 1980s, or the collapse of the Soviet Union in the 1990s, the IMF "has been enlisted largely because (a) it's there and (b) its resources are there."

Siddharth Tiwari, director of Strategy, Policy, and Review at the IMF, said, "in the way I think we are structured, we produce three public goods. One is surveillance. [Second] is capacity building. Third is financial support." IMF, he joked, has changed from meaning "It's Mostly Fiscal" to "It's Mostly Financial" as times have changed. Responding to a comment by Ted Truman about SDRs, he said that IMF resources have declined from the equivalent of 60 percent of gross member capital flows in 1970 to about 20 percent, so he saw a need for more resources, whether via a capital increase or issuing SDRs.

Responding to a question from **Randal Quarles, Tao Zhang,** China's executive director at the IMF, said that in his view, the buildup of foreign reserves in some countries and regional reserve lending arrangements or swap lines between central banks were adaptative responses. The IMF's nearly universal membership, highly trained staff, and experience with surveillance makes it advantageous for some kinds of international cooperation, but that does not preclude cooperation by other groups perhaps better adapted to certain niches.

Quarles noted that the IMF's level of political input was both a source of legitimacy and a weakness in its activity and asked whether the IMF can "be sufficiently rules-based to limit moral hazard in a crisis." **David DeRosa,** in effect, said no, but what moral hazard there is comes mostly out of countries' own policies, not the behavior of the IMF. As for moral hazard in the sense of bailouts of investor, he said, "I don't believe so much in institutions. I like markets to set the tone and to do the rescuing." **The other panelists** agreed with DeRosa that no country gets into trouble simply to get an IMF loan. **Guillermo Ortiz** applauded the IMF's recent efforts to improve multilateral surveillance, which fill a gap apparent in its failure to flag the risks accumulating before the global financial crisis. **Siddharth Tiwari** remarked that a key function the IMF can perform that central banks and regional lending arrangements cannot as easily do is to provide an objective assessment of a country's credit.

Randal Quarles asked what role the IMF has in crisis prevention as opposed to crisis management. **Siddharth Tiwari** said, "It's clear there's no simple straightforward indicator of liquidity," but the IMF has begun to use some indicators in its work to assess vulnerabilities. **Tao Zhang** noted the difference between national crises that do not affect other countries and crises that affect multiple countries and raise issues of coordination. Providing liquidity through SDRs has potential as a tool of crisis prevention, but this is a matter for the future, not the present. **David DeRosa** noted that during the global financial crisis, the problem was not a generalized lack of liquidity, but specifically a lack of U.S. dollars. The Federal Reserve addressed the problem through swap lines with foreign central banks; the IMF's role was minor.

Randal Quarles asked, "Is there sufficient consensus on macroeconomic policy measures to give the role of evaluator or enforcer of macroeconomic policy measures to the Fund?" He also asked whether the IMF's government structure has political legitimacy. **Siddharth Tiwari** answered that the crisis splintered the consensus about what to do in crises, because of controversies over, for instance, monetary policy at the zero lower bound, but that the consensus about what to do in normal times remains intact. **Tao Zhang** agreed, but added that there has been consensus among IMF members about the value of IMF surveillance.

In comments and questions from the audience, **Otmar Issing,** former member of the Executive Board of the European Central Bank (ECB), commented that during his time at the Bundesbank and the ECB, IMF surveillance, he thought, was too U.S.-centric in its thinking and did not have a good understanding of the monetary strategies of those two organizations. **Barbara Matthews** of BCM International Regulatory Analytics suggested that "the Fund's biggest problem going into the next decade is that there is zero habit for cooperation and there is not a lot of political sentiment anywhere on the planet to engage in cooperative agreements." **Ted Truman** agreed with Matthews that the centrifugal forces were strong and that was why he was highly disappointed with the U.S. failure to approve a quota increase at the IMF.

Eric Stein of Eaton Vance asked whether the IMF creates moral hazard by lending to countries when it should not. **Charles Goodhart,** former member of the Bank of England's Monetary Policy Committee, asked whether the euro area's institutions have usurped what were formerly IMF roles, for instance, in the Greek crisis. **Domingo Cavallo,** former Argentine minister of the economy, defended the need for the IMF as a crisis lender.

Guillermo Ortiz and **David DeRosa** agreed that it was a mistake for the IMF to get involved in Greece in the way it did, as a junior partner. **Siddharth Tiwari** pointed out that working with common currency areas is different from one-currency, one-country situations, and that the IMF is "obliged to respond" to members in trouble, though it will set conditions on the financing.

Tao Zhang noted that the IMF quota structure has lagged behind shifts in the structure of the world economy, which affects its ability to be a focal point for cooperation. He also said that the IMF has become more transparent, which should help some with the point Eric Stein raised because it makes the IMF's thinking clearer to markets.

Ted Truman said that the IMF in fact does often say no to countries initially, then they return after their situation worsens and it lends to them then. On the Greek crisis, he said, "the mistake with Europe was the Fund didn't address that as a euro area crisis but rather than as a Greek crisis." **Guillermo Ortiz** said that it was a welcome development that the IMF now tailors its advice more to the situations of particular countries. He was also heartened by the IMF's efforts to integrate bilateral and multilateral surveillance to get a better picture of risks.

Paper: Critical Issues for the Bretton Woods Institutions

William Rhodes, President and CEO of William R. Rhodes Global Advisors, provided some thoughts about the challenges and opportunities for the IMF and World Bank.

He noted that the IMF and World Bank are not as paramount in the global economic system as formerly, because of the growth of private capital markets and the rise of institutions such as the regional development banks, the Group of 20, and the Financial Stability Board. "In addition, there is a fundamental challenge to the Bank and to the Fund, as they are perceived by many developing countries and emerging market countries as being dominated by the governments of the major industrial economies." The International Finance Corporation (IFC) "has been a major success story. But…is it using its official status to edge out meaningful private competition?"

Rhodes saw these as the core issues for the IMF and World Bank:

"On the World Bank first: It continues to lend to many countries that have very substantial reserves and strong access to the capital markets. It does so to ensure its large balance sheet and its powerful AAA status in the markets where it borrows. But, is it not time that this policy be thoroughly reviewed and that many current borrowers be graduated?…

"As we discuss this, however, we should note that the Bank's leadership had downplayed this role in recent times. The Bank frequently defines itself these days in terms of two related actions: '(i) ending extreme poverty by reducing the percentage of people living on less than \$1.25 a day to three percent (of the global population) by 2030; and (ii) promoting shared prosperity by fostering income growth for the bottom 40 percent of the population in every country.'

"In this context, the World Bank could be, perhaps, an increasingly powerful engine of technical assistance. It is the supreme leader in knowledge and research among the official development agencies and this is a role in which, as it considers specializing its focus more on absolute poverty, it could have still greater influence as a very active partner with other multilateral and bilateral aid agencies….

"Now, on the IMF: Today, the Fund is the lender of last resort for countries that have critical balance of payments problems. The influence the IMF has, despite its impressive research, and despite the learned discussions on the value of Article IV consultations, depends above all on how ill the patient is. Today, governments rarely go to the Fund for assistance unless they felt they had nowhere else to turn….

"I believe that ways need to be considered to strengthen the resources and the stature of the Fund so that it can play a more effective role as a crisis manager, as lender of last resort, as the critical actor in times of international crisis, and, very importantly, as a leader in preventing crises.

"I believe that the Fund should draw a lesson from its past successes in the 1980s, when in the midst of the Latin American debt crisis it moved rapidly to involve private financial institutions as partners in crisis management and crisis resolution situations.

"I would also suggest that the IMF should be playing a larger role in crisis prevention and here, too, the private sector should be an important partner.

"To a considerable degree the proliferation of institutions reflect concerns in the governments of a number of emerging markets over the power structures in the IMF and the World Bank. There is a strong feeling that the governance of these institutions, notably the allocation of voting rights, continues to greatly favor the United States and the traditional West European governments, while it fails to recognize the rise of the leading emerging market economies in the global economy....Until the governance issues are resolved, both the Bank and the IMF will suffer in their international standing and importance."

In response to an audience question from **Nancy Birdsall,** founding president of the Center of Global Development, **Rhodes** replied that the World Bank should retain its original mission as a credit cooperative and not just focus on eliminating poverty. **George Hogue** asked whether the IMF should be bigger, given that its resources are now far smaller in terms of world GDP and trade flows than originally. **Rhodes** implied yes, but stressed that the IMF should work more closely with the private sector on resolving actual or potential defaults. **Daniel Runde,** former director of the Office of Global Development Alliances at the U.S. Agency for International Development, asked Rhodes to elaborate on his critique of the IFC. **Rhodes** replied that "the IFC is basically intruding on the private sector," and "you really have to decide on what constitutes graduation" from access to the IFC.

In response to a question from a **Chinese** audience member, **Rhodes** noted that China wishes to have a larger role in the IMF and World Bank, commensurate with its increasing economic importance, and that unless the allocation of quotas at the IMF and World Bank changes, China will likely go its own way. Last, **Sean Hagan,** general counsel of the IMF, asked whether partnership between the IMF and the private sector is as feasible as in past debt crises, given that holdings of foreign debt are now widely dispersed, not just concentrated in a few commercial banks. **Rhodes** replied, "I'm an optimist on this. I think it can happen. It didn't happen too well in Greece, but it happened." He added, "I think a lot more can be done with collective action clauses going forward, and that would make a big difference."

Chapter 8
Conclusion and Steps Forward

Summary and Next Steps

Randal K. Quarles, former undersecretary for domestic finance of the U.S. Treasury Department and former U.S. executive director at the IMF, and CFS advisory board member, summarized the major themes of the conference with a cautionary note that the "discussions have been far too rich" and "far too high quality across far too many fronts for a recapitulation."

One theme was whether the increasing importance of China meant that the renminbi would soon become a major reserve currency. Quarles remarked that "there was a certain degree of consensus, as much as could be expected in a strong-minded group like this one, which I found surprising, that the answer was not much, and not soon. The extent of America's 'exorbitant privilege'" as the issuer of the leading reserve currency is less than often thought.

Another theme was liquidity in the regulation of financial institutions, of course, but also in the management of the international financial system more broadly: how to measure it, how to provide it and limit it appropriately on the level of individual financial institutions and the financial system, and how to coordinate international efforts concerning it. Thinking about liquidity leads to consideration of leverage, also widely discussed at this conference. Paul Tucker, Quarles related, explained how, before the global financial crisis, regulation had permitted debt to tangible equity ratios of up to 200 to 1. "[A] corollary of that insight is that the required changes in the capital regulatory system are necessarily effecting a dramatic reduction in the financing capacity of a given level of capital....The new system is requiring 10 to 12 times as much capital as banks, particularly in Europe, had been operating on to support their current asset level." Quarles reflected on Charles Goodhart's thoughts stating that "regulators have insufficiently focused on the fact that there are two ways to increase a fraction. You can raise the numerator, the capital, but you can also reduce the denominator, assets. And where the required change in the numerator is so great, the second is much easier than the first without some substantial incentives to do otherwise." Significant discussion, noted Quarles, was devoted to the importance of analyzing national balance sheets, which measure stocks of assets, in addition to GDP, capital movements, and other flow measures, when analyzing imbalances.

A final important thread that ran through many of the panels was the debate on rules versus discretion in monetary policy and financial regulation. "But unlike some of these other threads, it was more implicit than articulated, but in the end, I think it's one of the most important of the common elements that have characterized our discussions," Quarles pointed out; it's been a prominent point of contention regarding financial system policy for the last 20 years. In monetary policy, John Taylor, one of the best-known advocates of rules, discussed a "Near Internationally Cooperative Equilibrium" or NICE domestically driven rules-based policy at the beginning of the conference. On the other hand, Paul Tucker argued at this conference for a large measure of regulatory discretion because participants in financial markets can be quite ingenious in finding loopholes for regulatory arbitrage.

Quarles described this debate as "the fundamental issue in the regulation of the international financial architecture in the post-crisis world. And which side we come down on—and we have not yet come down on a side—will shape the world we live in more than any other issue, including some that have received far more focus for the next generation. We didn't solve that issue in our time here in New Hampshire, but the discussions deepened and sharpened this debate among many others, and given the nature of the participants here, will contribute importantly toward the ultimate outcome, whether for good or ill."

Quarles added, "One final reflection: Nearly every panel has had some discussions of the implications of this site, from the rooms in which we've slept, each identified with a delegate in 1944, to the remembrances of the descendants of the original participants, three of whom have been with us in the last two days, down to the copies of the daily updates of the war in 1944 that were distributed on our tables and were distributed to the people in this room 70 years ago. The conference has been informed by history. Now everyone here has a lot of our psyches tied up in being disciplined professionals. We are expert in the arcane of the financial sector. We are rigorous in our pursuit of precise analysis, and relentless in our unsentimental adherence to the view that the only way to make the world better is to be strictly driven by things as they are.

"But a final theme that has run through our deliberations here…is that it's possible even for such hard-bitten cases as ourselves to be inspired, to be inspired by this beautiful place, and to be inspired by the history of which our presence here makes us a part. And I do hope that the inspiration that's helped inform our discussions here carries forward with us as we go forward, and informs our continuing engagement on these issues in the coming months and years, and that we, like the people who were in this room 70 years ago will be mindful of the Greek proverb that:

"A society grows great when old people plant trees whose shade they know they will never sit in."

Is There a Future for International Cooperation?

Following an introduction by Mexico's former minister of finance and former governor of the Bank of Mexico **Guillermo Ortiz,** former Mexican president **Ernesto Zedillo** (whose achievements, as Ortiz noted, include a Ph.D. in economics from Yale University) gave the concluding formal address of the conference.

Zedillo noted that early in his career he had worked both for Ortiz and Ambassador Francisco Suárez Davila. He noted the important part that Suárez's father, Eduardo Suárez Aránzolo, had played at the 1944 Bretton Woods conference, and the debt that we owe to the statesmen of that era for creating "an international system that notwithstanding its imperfections helped to make the second half of the 20th century a radically different experience from the first part, so full of horrendous and shameful human and economic tragedies."

Zedillo struck a pessimistic note, however, at the way in which global cooperation has evolved over the last 20 or so years. He said, "I submit that only during the very acute phase [of the Great Recession] did the system rise to the occasion, and that this is not enough to declare victory. I do believe that the record of international economic cooperation has been quite spotty for many years, and particularly insufficient, and at best, erratic, precisely since contemporary globalization significantly intensified during the last decade of the past century."

Already in the first half of the 1990s, "there were authoritative voices that while celebrating the deepening of globalization also warned that it would come with new risks that unquestionably warranted a serious enhancement of international cooperation." Financial crises in Mexico (1994-95), East Asia (1997-98), Russia (1998), Brazil (1999), and Argentina (2001) were warnings that "should have sufficed to provide the necessary stimulus to close the rapidly growing governance gap."

There were, in fact, efforts to rise to the challenge. Stanley Fischer and Anne Krueger, as first deputy managing directors of the IMF, talked of making the IMF a true international lender of last resort and giving it an enhanced role in cases of sovereign debt restructuring. Talk of a "new international financial architecture" was rife. In November 2001, the members of the World Trade Organization launched the Doha Round of tariff reductions and admitted China. The consensus reached at the United Nations International Conference on Financing for Development in Monterrey, Mexico, in March 2002 furthered momentum. Leaders of many countries, both developed and developing, endorsed the consensus, which "spoke very clearly of the importance of improving global economic governance, of a strong coordination of macroeconomic policies, of the need to ensure that the IMF had a suitable array of financial facilities and resources to response to financial crisis, and of a strengthening of even that international tax cooperation."

Then momentum ceased. Capital flows, instead of moving from advanced to developing countries, now went in the other direction. Macroeconomic imbalances built up in the United States and within the euro area. National policymakers were complacent, despite efforts by the IMF to call attention to global imbalances.

The onset of the financial crisis in September 2008 galvanized the Group of 20 (G20) countries, which acknowledged in their November 2008 meeting that inconsistent and insufficiently coordinated policies had led to the crisis. "On that occasion, and in subsequent two meetings, they made concrete commitments to remedy the purported lack of cooperation by rightly focusing on financial reform, preservation of open markets, reinforcement of multilateral institutions, and certainly macroeconomic policy coordination.

Unfortunately, the impetus of 2008 and 2009 was seriously diminished by the time of the fourth and fifth summits in Toronto and Seoul, and practically extinguished by the Cannes meeting of late 2011."

Zedillo criticized the "rather Chaplinesque management by European leaders of their crisis" and the "rather Marxist approach in U.S. fiscal policy, particularly [from] the U.S. Congress. And, of course, I speak of Groucho Marx, not of Karl Marx." He added, "But perhaps nothing else highlights how much disregard there is for multilateral endeavors in some quarters of this great land, the birthplace of the United Nations and the Bretton Woods institutions, than the repeated failure by the U.S. Congress to ratify the capital increase for the IMF, agreed in principle by the G20 in April of 2009, and formally in 2010."

Some observers have proposed that there is contradiction among the goals of sovereignty, national democracy, and deep globalization, and that we can have at most two out of the three. Zedillo countered, "I am much more of the old persuasion that rather than an impossible trinity, the three conditions constitute three pillars that, if well placed, can provide a stronger foundation for international peace, security, and prosperity. The work of placing well those pillars must start by giving up any notion of absolute supremacy in the value of any of those pillars.

"Macroeconomic policy coordination to achieve higher growth while preventing the reappearance of unsustainable imbalances is the most urgent task. But this objective would hardly be achievable without the proper reforms to repower the Bretton Woods institutions in particular the IMF. As this conference has shown, there is no lack of ideas on how to pursue those endeavors. However, from experience, including the G20's disappointing performance, we know that achieving the kind of international cooperation warranted by the nature of contemporary challenges is by no means easy.

"Let us hope that in the not-too-distant future, political leaders will have the wisdom and courage to embark on the necessary construction without waiting for the sort of horrendous tragedies that preceded and stimulated the Bretton Woods conference seven decades ago."

Envoi: Thoughts on World War II in July 1944

To close the conference, **Carole Brookins,** former U.S. executive director of the World Bank Group, offered brief thoughts on the context of the 1944 Bretton Woods conference.

Delegates from 44 nations came to Bretton Woods on July 1, 1944, "with a vision and a great purpose to structure an international monetary system with both foresight and commitment, and they did this amidst a global war where uncertainty reigned, and the victory of those united nations was still a hope and hardly a reality.

"Just think about it. Half of them came from countries which were in war zones or at risk. Many of their families were at risk—they had family in military service, or living in occupied countries and didn't know if they would be able to return—and many were not able to return. Perhaps General Dwight Eisenhower, Supreme Allied Commander of the Atlantic front, while not speaking directly of Bretton Woods at the time, best described the purpose of those delegates. I'll quote him: 'Together we must learn how to compose differences, not with arms, but with intellect and decent purpose.'

"The Bretton Woods monetary conference planning was underway during major preparations for D-Day in the spring of 1944. When the allies landed in Normandy on D-Day, June 6, a foothold was established in Europe, but the battle of the Normandy Hedgerows was being waged brutally and indecisively, I might add, during June's planning conference in Atlantic City and throughout the time of the Bretton Woods conference in July....

"While delegates here were negotiating the terms of this Bretton Woods agreement, the war was raging.... July was the beginning of the end of Nazi control of France, when the allies broke out beyond the coastal areas to Central France, liberated Paris on August 25, and began their further eastward advance into Germany. At the same time, the Russian Army's Operation Bagration was the war's largest campaign on the eastern front, with the taking of the Baltic States by July 17, which, again, changed the fate of people representing their countries at this conference. And the Pacific Campaign also gained momentum following the Battle of the Philippine Seas, June 19 and 20. U.S. Marines landed on Saipan on June 15 but fought until July 9 to secure the island and raise the U.S. flag. Saipan was part of the brilliant U.S. island-hopping strategy, and was followed then by Guam, which led Allied forces to Japan and, thank God, the ultimate end of the Pacific War.

"It makes one most humble to consider the breadth of issues and challenges facing leaders in 1944 and those remarkable people who came here to Bretton Woods. The leaders in 1944 were charged with conducting this global war on both civilian and military fronts, yet they rose to greatness in service, and gave us this world that President Zedillo spoke about in his powerful remarks today.

"We all often raise the question—our friends ask it as well—and we discuss it amongst ourselves: 'Where are the great leaders with vision and purpose today?' President Zedillo's insights tonight give me confidence that 'yes, we do have leaders with vision and purpose today.' In laying out the many challenges we face, we now have 'marching orders' for going forward. So, our purpose here at Bretton Woods is not only to remember and honor those founders for what they had the courage to do, but more importantly to pick up the baton that they have given us and lead the system forward for the next 70 years."

List of Papers and Panels

Full papers and photographs from the "Bretton Woods: The Founders and the Future" conference can be found at the Center for Financial Stability's web site, www.centerforfinancialstability.org/bw2014.php

Chapter 1

Lawrence Goodman, "A Bretton Woods Now Would Be Impossible" and "Lessons from the Summer of 1944"

Jacques de Larosière, "Welcoming Message"

Eric Helleiner, Eric Rauchway, and Kurt Schuler, "What Have We Learned from Recent Research on Bretton Woods?"

Spencer F. Eccles, "Marriner Eccles: Father of the Modern Federal Reserve"

Francisco Suárez Dávila, "Mexico's Role at Bretton Woods: An Assessment 70 Years Later"

Chapter 2

Otmar Issing, "Future Prospects for the World's Foreign Exchange Rate System: Political Design vs. Evolution"

John B. Taylor, "NICE-Squared—Near an Internationally Cooperative Equilibrium"

LIU Mingkang, "A Few Thoughts on the Current International Monetary System"

Charles Goodhart, "The 1944 Keynes Plan: An Idea Whose Time Has Now Returned?"

Panel: Guillermo Ortiz (moderator), Peter Garber, Ronald McKinnon, and YU Yongding, "The International Monetary System: Alternative Perspectives and Prospects"

Chapter 3

Panel: Yves-André Istel (moderator), Adnan Akant, Takatoshi Ito, and Richard Portes, "Future Challenges for Advanced Economy Reserve Currencies"

Panel: Eduardo Aninat (moderator), Domingo Cavallo, Edward Offenbacher, and QIAO Yide, "Emerging Markets: New Reserve Currencies and Spillovers from Advanced Economies"

Chapter 4
Panel: Robin Lumsdaine (moderator), Sheila Bair, Charles Goodhart, and Richard Sandor, "The Future of Finance and Financial Institutions"

Panel: Jack Malvey (moderator), Peter N. Johnson, Stephen Kealhofer, and Dexter Senft, "Technology and the Future of the International Financial System"

Chapter 5
Panel: Lawrence Goodman (moderator), Robert Aliber, Nick Sargen, and Paul Tucker, "How to Better Anticipate and Manage Future Crises"

Panel: Robert Gray (moderator), Whitney Debevoise II, Sean Hagan, and Richard Portes, "The Future of Sovereign Debt Restructuring"

Chapter 6
Panel: Carole Brookins (moderator), Nancy Birdsall, Franco Passacantando, and Peter Woicke, "The Future Role of the World Bank"

Chapter 7
William Rhodes, "Critical Issues for the Bretton Woods Institutions"

Panel: Randal K. Quarles (moderator), David DeRosa, Siddharth Tiwari, Edwin (Ted) Truman, and Tao Zhang, "The Future Role of the IMF"

Chapter 8
Randal K. Quarles, "Summary and Next Steps"

Ernesto Zedillo, "In Light of Recent Experiences: Is There a Future for International Cooperation?"

Carole Brookins, "Thoughts on World War II in July 1944"

Delegates

We give only the briefest biographies of the delegates; further details about almost all are easy to find online. Affiliations were those as of the time of the conference except as noted.

Adnan Akant is Head of Foreign Exchange at Fischer Francis Trees and Watts.

Robert Albertson is Principal and Chief Strategist of Sandler O'Neill.

Robert Aliber is coauthor, with the late Charles Kindleberger, of the renowned *Manias, Panics, and Crashes: A History of Financial Crises.*

Eduardo Aninat was Deputy Managing Director of the IMF from 1999 to 2003.

Madelyn Antoncic is Vice President and Treasurer of the World Bank.

Claudio Antonini was Director at AlixPartners.

Sheila Bair was Chair of the Federal Deposit Insurance Corporation from 2006 to 2011.

Andreas Bauer is Head of Strategy, Policy and Review Department at the International Monetary Fund.

Nancy Birdsall is Founding President of the Center for Global Development.

Stanley Black is Georges Lurcy Distinguished Professor of Economics at University of North Carolina, Chapel Hill.

Bradley Bondi is Senior Fellow at the CFS and Partner, Cahill Gordon & Reindel.

Jennifer Borggaard is Senior Vice President at Affiliated Managers Group.

Bill Bradley was U.S. Senator and former candidate for the Democratic nomination for President.

Rebecca Braeu is Director of Sovereign Research for Standish Mellon Asset Management.

Carole Brookins was U.S. Executive Director of the World Bank Group from 2001 to 2005.

Domingo Cavallo was Argentina's Minister of the Economy from 1991 to 1996 and in 2001.

Christopher Chapman is Managing Director and Portfolio Manager, Manulife Investment Management.

Warren Coats was Chief of Operations Division for Special Drawing Rights at the International Monetary Fund.

Whitney Debevoise II is Senior Partner at Arnold & Porter LLP.

Jacques de Larosière was Managing Director of the International Monetary Fund from 1978 to 1987.

David DeRosa is President of DeRosa Research and Trading.

Spencer F. Eccles is Chairman Emeritus of Wells Fargo Intermountain Banking Region and Chairman of the Marriner Eccles Foundation.

Spencer P. Eccles is Co-founder and Managing Director of The Cynosure Group and Former Executive Director of the Office of Economic Development for Utah Governor Gary Herbert.

Barry Eichengreen is George C. Pardee and Helen N. Pardee Professor of Economics and Political Science at the University of California, Berkeley.

Joseph Engelhard is Senior Vice President at Capital Alpha Partners.

Rachel Evans is Reporter at Bloomberg News.

Roger E. A. Farmer is Distinguished Professor of Economics at University of California, Los Angeles.

John Feldmann is Senior Fellow at the CFS and a Macro Analyst at Discovery Capital Management.

Peter Garber is a Global Strategist at Deutsche Bank.

Atish Ghosh is Chief of the Systemic Issues Division and Assistant Director of the Research Department at the IMF.

Brenda Gonzalez-Hermosillo was Deputy Division Chief of the Global Financial Stability Division at the IMF.

Charles Goodhart was a Member of the Bank of England's Monetary Policy Committee from 1997 to 2000.

Lawrence Goodman is President of the Center for Financial Stability.

Deborah Green is Senior Researcher at Elliott Management.

Robert Gray is Chairman of Debt Finance and Advisory at HSBC Bank.

Mike Hanson is President and Chief Executive Officer of the Massachusetts Credit Union Share Insurance Corporation.

Sean Hagan was General Counsel and Director of the Legal Department at the International Monetary Fund.

Steve Hanke is a professor of applied economics and co-director of the Institute for Applied Economics, Global Health, and the Study of Business Enterprise at The Johns Hopkins University.

Zhiren He was a Ph.D. candidate at Shanghai Jiao Tong University.

Eric Helleiner is Professor in the Department of Political Science at the University of Waterloo (Ontario).

Patrice Hill was Chief Economic Correspondent at The Washington Times.

George R. Hoguet was Managing Director and Global Investment Strategist, State Street Global Advisors.

Haizhou Huang is Managing Director and Management Committee Member, China International Capital Corporation.

Otmar Issing was a Member of the Executive Board of the European Central Bank from 1998 to 2006.

Yves-André Istel is Senior Advisor and former Vice Chairman of Rothschild, Inc.

Takatoshi Ito was a Member of the Economic and Fiscal Council of the Japanese Ministry of Finance from 2006 to 2008.

Peter N. Johnson is Vice President of Enterprise Application and Information Services at MetLife.

Henry Kaufman is President of Henry Kaufman & Company.

Stephen Kealhofer is Managing Principal, Chief Risk Officer, and Co-founder of DCI.

Charles Kimball is Managing Director of Korea Center for International Finance.

Mahesh Kotecha is President and Founder of Structured Credit International Corporation.

Liu Mingkang was Chairman of the China Banking Regulatory Commission from 2003 to 2011 and Deputy Governor of the People's Bank of China from 2000 to 2002.

Jimmie Lenz was Chief Risk and Credit Officer at Well Fargo Advisors, LLC.

Roger Lowenstein is an author whose books include *America's Bank: The Epic Struggle to Create the Federal Reserve*, *The End of Wall Street*, *When Genius Failed*, and *Buffett*.

61

Robin Lumsdaine is Senior Fellow at CFS and Professor of International Finance at American University.

Michael Mackenzie was U.S. Markets Editor at the *Financial Times*.

Jack Malvey was Chief Global Markets Strategist, BNY Mellon.

Horacio Marquez was Member of the Board of Directors at OnePak, Inc.

David X. Martin is Special Counselor at the CFS and Cyber Risk Management Advisor.

Barbara Matthews was Founder of BCM International Regulatory Analytics.

Dick Mayo is Chairman of Mayo Capital Partners and was Founding Partner of Grantham, Mayo, Van Otterloo & Co.

Chris McAlister is Managing Director and Global Head of Trading at Prudential.

Robert McCauley was Senior Adviser and former Chief Representative for Asia and the Pacific, Bank for International Settlements.

Ronald McKinnon (1935-2014) was Professor of International Economics at Stanford University.

Matthew McLennan is Head of the Global Value Team at First Eagle Investment Management.

Stephen Miller was Financial Markets Scholar at the Mercatus Center.

Joel Motley was Managing Director at Public Capital Advisors and Chairman of the Governance Committee for Oppenheimer Funds.

Simon Nocera is Founder, Principal & Chief Investment Officer, Lumen Advisors.

Jens Nystedt was Portfolio Manager and Global Strategist at Moore Capital Management.

Edward Offenbacher is a Member of the Management Board of the Bank of Israel.

Guillermo Ortiz was Finance Minister of Mexico from 1994 to 1998 and Governor of the Bank of Mexico from 1998 to 2009.

Franco Passacantando was Executive Director and Dean of the World Bank Board of Directors from1995 to 2003.

Richard Portes is Professor of Economics at London Business School.

Qiao Yide is Vice Chairman and Secretary General of the Shanghai Development Research Foundation.

Randal K. Quarles was Under Secretary for Domestic Finance of the U.S. Treasury Department from 2005 to 2006.

William Rapp is Henry J. Leir Professor of International Trade and Business at the New Jersey Institute of Technology.

Eric Rauchway is Professor of History at the University of California-Davis.

William R. Rhodes is President and CEO of William R. Rhodes Global Advisors.

Dan Runde is Director of the Project on Prosperity and Development at the Center for Strategic and International Studies.

Richard L. Sandor is CEO of American Financial Exchange (AFX) and CFS Advisory Board Member.

Nick Sargen was Chief Economist of Fort Washington Investment.

Hilmar Schaumann was Chief Risk Officer of Fortress Investment Group.

Vicki Schmelzer was Senior FX Reporter at Market News International.

Charles Schott is Senior Advisor at CFS.

Kurt Schuler is Senior Fellow in Financial History at the Center for Financial Stability.

Anthony Segal-Knowles was Advisor to the International Monetary Fund in the United Kingdom.

Dexter Senft is Co-Head of Electronic Markets at Morgan Stanley.

Paul Sheard was the Chief Global Economist at Standard & Poor's.

Judy Shelton is Co-Director of the Sound Money Project at the Atlas Economic Research Foundation.

Rajiv Singh was Chief Executive Officer of Rabobank's North America Wholesale franchise.

Paul Speltz is Chairman and CEO of Global Strategic Associates.

Eric Stein was Vice President and Co-Director of the Global Income Group, Eaton Vance Management.

Arthur Steinmetz was President and Chief Executive Officer, Oppenheimer Funds.

Francisco Suárez Dávila was Ambassador of Mexico to Canada from 2013 to 2016.

John B. Taylor is Professor of Economics at Stanford University.

Landon Thomas was Economy and Finance Reporter for *The New York Times*.

Siddharth Tiwari is Director of Strategy, Policy, and Review at the International Monetary Fund.

Edwin (Ted) Truman is Senior Fellow at the Peterson Institute for International Economics.

Paul Tucker was a Member of the Monetary Policy of the Bank of England from 2009 to 2013 and Deputy Governor from 2009 to 2013.

Gertjan Vlieghe was Partner at Brevan Howard.

David Westbrook is Louis A. Del Cotto Professor and Director for Global Strategies Initiatives at SUNY Buffalo Law School.

James Winder was Senior Associate at the Cynosure Group.

Peter Woicke was Managing Director of the World Bank and CEO of the International Finance Corporation from 1999 to 2005.

Yu Yongding was a Member of the Monetary Policy Committee of the People's Bank of China from 2004 to 2006.

Ernesto Zedillo was President of Mexico from 1994 to 2000.

Zhang Tao is Deputy Managing Director at the International Monetary Fund.

Joshua Zumbrun was National Correspondent for *The Wall Street Journal.*

www.ingramcontent.com/pod-product-compliance
Lightning Source LLC
Chambersburg PA
CBHW070945210326
41520CB00021B/7068